The Lutheran Handbook for Pastors

About "Winking Luther"

Martin Luther's theology is grounded in paradoxes—sinner/saint, law/gospel, hidden/revealed—and illuminated by a down-to-earth, everyday sense of humor. This icon of Luther winking at the reader combines the serious, formal scholarship that was his life's work with the humor and lightheartedness that characterized his personality.

Nowhere is this combination more evident than in Luther's writings regarding the office of pastor, in which a light touch and sense of humor rise to the level of absolute necessity if one is to long endure. Luther's face here captures this sentiment. With a wink he extends to you, from one pastor to another, an invitation to an insider's "table talk" about the ups and downs of ministry. With plenty of helpful advice, of course.

The Lutheran Handbook
for Pastors

Augsburg Fortress
Minneapolis

New brand development editor: Kristofer Skrade
Editors: Gloria E. Bengtson, Laurie J. Hanson, James Satter, Rebecca Lowe
Cover designer: Laurie Ingram-Duren
Interior illustrator: Brenda Brown

Contributing writers: Paul J. Blom, Richard Bruesehoff, Eric Burtness, Lou Carlozo, Robert Buckley Farlee, Paul N. Hanson, Susan L. Houglum, Rolf A. Jacobson, Mark D. Johns, Ken Sundet Jones, James Kasperson, Charles R. Lane, Susan M. Lang, Beth A. Lewis, Catherine Malotky, Mark C. Mattes, Robin McCullough-Bade, Carolyn M. Mowchan, Paul J. Owens, Michael Rogness, Mitzie Spencer Schafer, Theodore W. Schroeder, Megan Torgerson, Thomas L. Weitzel, and Hans Wiersma

ISBN-13: 978-0-8066-5296-2
ISBN-10: 0-8066-5296-9

The paper used in this publication meets the minimum requirements of American National Standard for Information Sciences—Permanence of Paper for Printed Library Materials, ANSI Z329.48-1984.

Manufactured in the U.S.A.

10 09 08 07 06   1 2 3 4 5 6 7 8 9 10

CONTENTS

This Book Belongs to 11

Congregations Served 12

Preface 13

Call Stuff

How to Know if You're Called to Be a Pastor 16

Luther's Call to Ministry 18

How to Avoid Becoming the Pastor You Swore You'd Never Be and Become the Pastor You Always Wanted to Be 20

How to Manage Your Relationship with the Bishop 24

Five Important Ways the Lutheran Confessions Define Pastoral Ministry 27

Seven Things Luther and the Reformers Said about Ministry 30

How to Know When It's Time to Find a New Call 33

Seven Things to Keep in Mind When You Interview for a New Call 36

What to Do When You Question Whether You're the Right Person for the Call You're In 39

How to Retire from Ministry Gracefully 42

Administrative Stuff

Five Tips on Hiring the Right Personnel to Make a Great
Ministry Team 46

Thirty Subjects You Should Never Ask about When
Interviewing for New Staff 49

How to Empower Your Staff to Do Good Work 52

Five Things Senior Pastors Can Do to Endear Themselves
to Their Staff 55

How to Run a Staff Meeting 57

How to Fire Someone When You Really Have To 60

How to Get the Best Out of the Church Administrative
Assistant 63

How to Relate Effectively to a Senior Colleague 66

How to Relate Effectively to a Junior Colleague 67

Five Common Pitfalls Solo Pastors Fall Into and How
to Avoid Them 68

Ten Tips for Building Effective Pastoral Relationships
in a Congregation 71

Four Unlikely Leaders in the Bible and What You Can
Learn from Them 74

How to Release Your Congregation's Ability to Develop
a Vision for Ministry 77

How to Delegate 80

How to Enable Your Congregation to Live as the
Priesthood of All Believers 82

How to Participate in a Committee Meeting without
Having to Be in Charge   85

How to Take Charge of a Committee Meeting When
It Gets Off Track   87

How to Support and Empower the Church Council
without Becoming a Dictator or a Wallflower   89

How to Survive an Annual Meeting   92

Ten Things about Parish Ministry They Didn't Teach You
in Seminary   95

How to Read a Congregational Financial Statement
(and Why It's Important)   99

How to Manage Your Calendar   101

How to Carve Out Time for Sermon Preparation   103

How to Lead a Retreat   105

Pastoral Stuff

Luther's Five Biggest Pastoral Dilemmas and How
He Handled Them   110

How to Follow Jesus as Your Pastoral Model   112

How and When to Respond to a Request for
Pastoral Care   115

How to Make an Effective Hospital Visit   117

How to Make an Effective Home Visit   119

How to Make an Effective Shut-in and Care
Facility Visit   121

Ten Things You Should Never Say to a Parishioner 123

How to Use the Grapevine to Support Your Ministry 126

How to Identify a Church Alligator 128

How to Avoid Getting Triangulated 130

How to Manage Habitual Drop-in Visitors so You Can
Get Your Work Done 132

How to Remain Calm in a Crisis Situation 134

How to Prepare Mentally for a Funeral 136

Seven Preachers in the Bible and What Made
Them Great 138

How to Preach a Prophetic Word without Getting Fired 141

Three Jokes for Use with Church Crowds 143

How to Preach a Stewardship Sermon without
Sounding Like You Are Begging for a Raise 145

How to Create a Climate of Care, Love, and Openness
in Your Congregation 147

How to Conduct Yourself at an Ecumenical Worship
Service 150

How to Deal with Disgruntled Transfers from
Other Churches 152

How to Drink Coffee 154

How to Accept Cookies and Other Goodies Graciously
without Gaining Weight 157

How to Listen to the Same Story for the 100th Time
and Feign Interest   160

How to Respond When You Forget a Parishioner's Name   161

Four Ways to Handle the Tacky Gifts that Parishioners
Give You   163

Worship Stuff

Ten Things You Should Never Say During Worship   166

How to Welcome Visitors   168

How to Use Your Family Members as Sermon
Illustrations without Alienating Them or Boring
the Congregation   169

How to Preach without Notes   172

How to Wing a Sermon When You Forget Your Notes
at Home   174

Eight Common Hand Gestures Used in Preaching   176

Nine Uses for Old Sermon Manuscripts   179

How to Recover When You Lose Your Place or Forget
During a Public Presentation   181

How to Recruit Worship Assistants Discreetly When
Someone Doesn't Show Up   183

How to Handle a Ringing Cell Phone during Worship   185

How to Handle Loudspeaker Feedback   187

How to Recover from an Open-Mike Gaffe   189

How to Respond to a Shrieking Child Incident   191

Five Common Wedding Faux Pas and How
to Avoid Them   193

How to Survive an Anxious Bridal Party   195

Personal Stuff

How to Recover from Christmas and Easter Overload   198

How to Stay Fit   201

How to Establish and Maintain the Discipline of Daily
Devotions   204

How to Keep Up on Current Trends in Theology,
Even When You're Busy   206

How to Maintain a Social Life as a Single Pastor   208

How to Keep Both Your Job and Your Family   210

Five Ways to Help Your Marriage Thrive Despite
the Demands of the Job   212

How to Avoid Answering Personal Questions   214

How to Get Out of a Traffic Ticket   216

The Pros and Cons of Wearing a Clergy Shirt   219

This Book Belongs to

Name _____

Address _____

_____

E-mail _____

Telephone _____

Birth date _____

Birthplace _____

Baptismal date _____

Place of baptism _____

Congregations Served

Name _____

My favorite story from this congregation _____

_____

_____

Name _____

My favorite story from this congregation _____

_____

_____

Name _____

My favorite story from this congregation _____

_____

_____

Name _____

My favorite story from this congregation _____

_____

_____

Name _____

My favorite story from this congregation _____

_____

_____

PREFACE

Please Be Advised:

Few professions call upon a wider range of skills, demand more of you personally, or offer as many unique rewards as that of pastor. Whatever the "parish" you serve happens to be—large congregation or small, student body, hospital, military base, synod, long-term care facility, or whatever—you know this to be true: pastoral ministry is a multifaceted challenge with no shortage of difficulties. One thing all pastors seem to agree upon is that if you want to survive ordained ministry you're going to need a robust sense of humor. Without one you're sunk.

Lots of books have been written over the years to address the challenges you face in ministry. Some fall into the self-help category and are filled with good information to help ward off burnout, workaholism, despair, and whatnot. Other books take a more positive, proactive tack and aim at providing good models for pastors, everything from Jesus himself to notable business leaders like Warren Buffett or Lee Iacocca. Some even cast Jesus as a business leader, giving him the veneer of a sharp suit and tie, all to varying degrees of success. Still others seem to want the role to be elevated to a higher plane than other vocations, and not merely "set apart" as the word *ordo* would suggest.

The little volume you now hold in your hands takes a slightly different approach from these. Its predecessor, *The Lutheran Handbook,* focused on Lutheran culture and theology, while *The Lutheran Handbook for Pastors* peels back the veil from this most holy and earthy profession to reveal everyday situations that every pastor encounters and to provide some helpful tips for coping. But these tips are offered with a healthy dose of humor (delivered wryly, of course, with tongue firmly planted in cheek), because the call to pastoral ministry, while holy and sacramental, must nevertheless be undertaken in the flesh—a flesh that is itself prone to human sin.

If you, dear reader, happen to not be a pastor, it is our fervent hope that you will catch an illuminative glimpse of the obedient life and thereby gain some new appreciation for this rarified role and the vagaries to which its members are subjected.

Being a pastor, of course, is not all pain and suffering. Far from it. For one thing, your medical and dental insurance is excellent. For another, you can get away with wearing a clergy shirt upwards of 10 times without washing it, as long as you wear some kind of undershirt. And perhaps equal to these benefits is the constant knowledge that your job—this profession of planting seeds and patiently waiting for the growth—is all about the transcendent, transformative Word, Jesus Christ, who changes lives and brings us all into alignment with God.

—Kristofer Skrade

CALL STUFF

HOW TO KNOW IF YOU'RE CALLED TO BE A PASTOR

The call to be a pastor has two parts: an internal call and an external call. You need both to be one of the church's public proclaimers of the gospel.

❶ The inner call. (You may be called to ordained ministry if...)

- You are a sinner, and Christ forgives your sin (which he does).

- You regularly seek out Christ's benefits in Word and sacrament, because without them you have nothing.

- You can't help telling others about your Lord, now that you know how deeply your sin and Christ's mercy run in you.

- You read and pray and think and learn so that you become steeped in the strong vocabulary of faith.

- You find that your will is no longer your own because it is shaped by the cross.

- You develop a callus from shaking hands on Sunday mornings.

- You can ingest large quantities of low-grade coffee without becoming ill.

- You weep openly whenever you sing "A Mighty Fortress Is Our God."

❷ The external call. (You may be called to ordained ministry if...)

- The church has called you to speak God's Word in the world.

- You have been given a letter of call.
- You smile and reflexively extend your right hand at the approach of another person.

Please Note

- Lay leaders and pastors might encourage you to consider ordained ministry and assist you in discerning and affirming the internal call.

- You can explore your vocation in general and the call to public ministry in particular with the help of your congregation, Bible camp, campus ministry, or synod. Synod staff will also work with you in the candidacy process.

- There are situations in which either the church or you yourself may determine that you are no longer called to be a pastor. At that point you may no longer function in the role of pastor, but like every baptized Christian you will remain called to give witness to your Lord in your daily life.

LUTHER'S CALL TO MINISTRY

1 In January 1505, Martin Luther earned his master's degree from the University of Erfurt, Germany, ranking second in his class. Then he entered law school at Erfurt and bought books for his legal studies.

2 In June, Luther made a trip to Mansfeld to visit his parents.

3 In early July, on the way back to Erfurt, Luther found himself in the middle of a violent thunderstorm. Fearing for his life, Luther cried out, "Help, St. Anne! I'll become a monk!"

4 Luther survived the thunderstorm and kept his vow, entering the Augustinian Monastery in Erfurt on July 17, 1505. His law books were returned to the book-seller.

Please Note

- Luther later understood that since fear of God (rather than love for God) motivated him to join the priesthood, his decision to become a monk was worthless. Nevertheless, in hindsight, Luther was able to see the hand of God at work in his less-than-admirable call to ministry. That is, Luther's call may have been lacking in proper motivation but, as Luther himself put it, "See how much good the merciful Lord has allowed to come of it."

- Think safety first. Seek shelter at the first sign of a severe storm. Not every incidence of thunder and lightning indicates a call to ministry.

Mansfeld
(Home of Luther's parents)

Stotternheim
(Where lightning struck)

Erfurt
(Locale of University of Erfurt Law School, as well as the Augustinian Monastery.)

HOW TO AVOID BECOMING THE PASTOR YOU SWORE YOU'D NEVER BE AND BECOME THE PASTOR YOU ALWAYS WANTED TO BE

You are not hired for a leadership role as much as you're called to live out an "office"—the Office of Word and Sacrament. In the Ordination Service, you make three promises describing three dimensions of this office: preacher, pastor, and person. These do's and don'ts will help you avoid becoming the pastor you swore you'd never be and become the pastor you always wanted to be.

❶ You are a preacher. ("Will you preach and teach in accordance with the Holy Scriptures, the creeds, and the Lutheran Confessions?")
Speech is often considered to be "mere words." But words have real power to bind and to free, to kill and to raise up. What you say has great effect.

Don't:

- Talk about yourself in sermons, except when making a point about sin—never as a hero or martyr.
- Talk in general terms about Jesus or salvation, as in "Jesus loves sinners" or "Jesus died for us."

Do:

- Talk about Jesus. He is the hero; he is the faithful one. Preach like John the Baptist who said, "He must increase, but I must decrease" (John 3:30).
- Take the gospel to your listeners by saying "for you," as in "Jesus loves you" and "Jesus died for you."

Don't underestimate the tools of your trade: the Word, prayer, and the sacraments. No one else has tools like these.

❷ You are a pastor. ("Will you pray for God's people, and nourish them with the Word and Holy Sacraments?")

"Pastor" can mean "shepherd," one who watches over the flock, the congregation.

Don't:

- Worry too much about keeping people happy. The word "happy" appears nowhere in your letter of call, and this doesn't just apply to you yourself.

- Underestimate the tools of your trade: the Word, prayer, and the sacraments. These are not second best. No physician, counselor, or guru offers these life-giving things.

Do:

- Remember the difference between who you serve and who you work for. You serve the congregation, but you work for God.

- Stick to the basics. People need what pastors provide—a word from God, prayers, and dependable sacramental promises.

❸ You are a person. ("Will you lead by your own example in faithful service and holy living? Will you give faithful witness in the world, that God's love may be known in all you do?")

Don't:

- Be phony. You are holy only because Christ makes you holy.

- Be one-dimensional. There's more to life than church stuff.

Do:

- Be real. It's okay to be a human being. Relax. Play. Life is short.
- Have a life. That's what Christ has freed you for. Know your family. Stay healthy.
- Pick one time-management tool and use it.

Please Note

- God will answer your prayer. At ordination, when asked if you will be a faithful preacher, pastor, and person, you respond: "I will, and I ask God to help me." God will help you, and will make of you the pastor you always wanted to be.

HOW TO MANAGE YOUR RELATIONSHIP WITH THE BISHOP

1 Become familiar with the Office of the Bishop and its responsibilities, as assigned in the Constitution of the Church.

Note that a pastor in any Word and Sacrament call would have many of the same responsibilities (for example, preaching, teaching, leading worship, and celebrating the sacraments). The bishop's primary role, however, is to "oversee" the mission and ministry of the whole church body in relationship to both the synod and the wider expressions of the church.

2 Become acquainted with the person called to this office.

Intentionally cultivate a relationship of trust with this person. Get to know her or his likes and dislikes. In conversation, clarify your expectations of the bishop's role in your own ministry and life. Consider finding out the brand of your bishop's favorite candy and send him or her a case of it, especially if you might enter the mobility process in the near future.

3 Advocate for the synod's ministry and mission in support of the bishop and staff.

If you do not agree with some of the bishop's proposals, take time to sit down and discuss the matter in person. Have some constructive suggestions ready to address the issues.

❹ Challenge rumors and gossip about the bishop's work when you encounter them.

Remind people that there is likely much more to the situation than is known publicly. Recognize that bishops are not called to "fix" things, but can only provide guidance, leadership, and recommendations in the process of addressing problems.

❺ Invite the bishop and staff to worship with your congregation occasionally.

Do not wait for the bishop to simply show up unannounced, since they hardly ever do that. More often than

Don't surprise your bishop. Keep the bishop informed about how things are going in your setting and, when necessary, your personal life.

not, the bishop's calendar is filled a number of months in advance, so extend the invitation with plenty of lead time. Consider renting a red carpet and trumpet choir for the occasion.

⑥ Don't surprise your bishop.
Keep the bishop informed about how things are going in your own setting and in your personal life. If problems arise, inform the bishop so he or she can pray for and with you, as well as provide care and assistance to you and your setting or family.

⑦ Shake hands with the bishop.
Use good manners. Greet the bishop with a firm handshake.

FIVE IMPORTANT WAYS THE LUTHERAN CONFESSIONS DEFINE PASTORAL MINISTRY

1 Word and Sacrament ministry exists to create and further faith.

So that we may obtain this faith, the ministry of teaching the gospel and administering the sacraments was instituted. For through the Word and the sacraments as through instruments the Holy Spirit is given, who effects faith where and when it pleases God.

—The Augsburg Confession (1530), *Book of Concord*, p. 41

2 Word and Sacrament ministry leads people to look to God as the source of all good.

To have a God, as you can well imagine, does not mean to grasp him with your fingers, or to put him into a purse, or to shut him up in a box. Rather, you lay hold of God when your heart grasps him and clings to him. To cling to him with your heart is nothing else than to entrust yourself to him completely. He wishes to turn us away from everything else apart from him, and to draw us to himself, because he is the one, eternal good.

—The Large Catechism (1529), *Book of Concord*, p. 388

3 Word and Sacrament ministry shapes the good news, acting as God's mouthpiece.

The Father draws people by the power of his Holy Spirit through the hearing of his holy, divine Word, as with a net, through which the elect are snatched out of the jaws of the devil. For this reason every poor sinner should

act in such a way as to hear the Word diligently and not doubt that the Father is drawing people to himself.
—Solid Declaration, Formula of Concord (1577), *Book of Concord*, pp. 652–653

❹ Word and Sacrament ministry teaches the faith, especially to the young and to those new to the faith. Therefore, my dear sirs and brothers, who are either pastors or preachers, I beg all of you for God's sake to take up your office boldly, to have pity on your people who are

As a pastor, you are God's mouthpiece, sharing the good news.

entrusted to you, and to help us bring the catechism to the people, especially to the young.
—The Small Catechism, *Book of Concord*, p. 348

⑤ Word and Sacrament ministry offers the healing power of confession.
Rather we give this advice: If you are poor and miserable, then go and make use of the healing medicine. Those who feel their misery and need will no doubt develop such a desire for confession that they will run to it with joy.
—The Large Catechism, *Book of Concord*, p. 479

SEVEN THINGS LUTHER AND THE REFORMERS SAID ABOUT MINISTRY

❶ Ministry is God's business.
Because God saves by faith in Christ, sinners need a way to get that faith. Article 5 of the Augsburg Confession says, "So that we may obtain this faith, the ministry of teaching the gospel and administering the sacraments was instituted" (*Book of Concord*, p. 41). When Melanchthon defined the Office of Ministry, he never mentioned pastors, because the ministry of word and sacrament is God's way of saving sinners.

❷ The center of ministry is forgiveness for sinners.
Article 28 of the Augsburg Confession argues that what sinners need is the announcement that they are freely forgiven on account of Christ (*Book of Concord*, p. 289).

❸ Pastoral ministry is hard work.
You can't be an effective public proclaimer of the gospel if you expect an easy ride. Yet even though there's little thanks involved, Christ himself is your reward (Small Catechism, *Book of Concord*, p. 351).

❹ Ministry involves teaching and learning.
"There is no doctrine which ought to be learned more diligently than the knowledge of eternal salvation. Therefore with burning zeal and diligent care we must produce teaching methods and catechisms in the churches which surpass those used elsewhere" (Martin Bucer, De regno

Christi, in *Melanchthon and Bucer*, ed. by Wilhelm Pauck, Philadelphia: Westminster Press, 1969, p. 234).

⑤ God sustains the call to ministry.
"The chief thing of the ministry is that God wants to be present in it with His Spirit, grace, and gifts and to work effectively through it. But God wants to give increase to the planting and watering of those who have been legitimately called to the ministry...that both they themselves and others might be saved" (Martin Chemnitz, *Ministry,*

God needs the best and the brightest for pastoral ministry.

Word, and Sacraments: An Enchiridion, trans. by Luther Poellot, St. Louis: Concordia, 1981, pp. 29-30).

⑥ Ministry requires the best and brightest.
Effectiveness in ministry lies in more than personal piety. In preparing people to assess the state of the church in Saxony, Melanchthon said bishops should "question and examine" a prospective pastor "so that by God's help we may carefully prevent any ignorant or incompetent person from being accepted and unlearned folk being misled. For time and again...experience has shown how much good or evil may be expected from competent or incompetent preachers."

⑦ Pastors need to know exactly what ministry consists of.
When candidates for ministry were tested by their professors before being sent into a call, they had to be able to give an exact description of the content of ministry: "The office of preaching is a command which God has given with explicit words: to preach the holy gospel, to deliver the sacraments, to forgive sins,...to chastise sins, but just with God's word and not by worldly power. And if God is to be powerful through this office, he will give the forgiveness of sins, the Holy Spirit, life and comfort and eternal blessedness" (Philip Melanchthon, *Examen ordinandorum*).

HOW TO KNOW WHEN IT'S TIME TO FIND A NEW CALL

It's probably not good to wait until someone says, "If you're ever looking for a truck you can use for moving, mine's available." Or, as you're returning from vacation you hear, "Oh, were you gone?" or "Are you back already?" So what should you pay attention to?

❶ Listen to your heart.
Remind yourself of the passion and joy you felt when you began this call. If it's been replaced by indifference or cynicism, pay attention.

❷ Consider the renewing nature of your current call.
It's not unusual, since passion comes and goes, to find yourself called to the same place again—several times. Stay with it. You'll learn to tell the difference between your own version of temporary and long-term indifference.

❸ Assess and reassess your gifts and skill set and the congregation's needs.
Congregations change. Communities change. Pastors change. Your evolved or evolving gifts may not be what the congregation now needs, and vice versa. Another congregation may be looking for what you're good at!

❹ You keep opening doors, but there's someone behind you closing them.
Doing ministry is hard work. Together with the congregation you've worked through obstacles and done good things. However, sometimes congregations just want to

rest for a spell. Or they want to be engaged in God's mission in a new way.

If people say "Oh, were you gone?" or "Are you back already?" as you return from vacation, it may be past time to look for a new call.

⑤ You detect a call from another place.

You've been minding your own ministry, but other congregations have heard about you. Synod staff members have noticed you. Paying attention to their interest in you—maybe even agreeing to an interview—may help you to clarify your call situation.

⑥ Find someone to walk with you.

Talk with your family, and recognize that they have their own interest in the decision too, then find someone whose real interest is walking with you as you do your discerning. Avoid involving members of your current congregation.

Please Note

- Sometimes, even if you're not ready to go or your family's not ready to go, it may still be time to look for a new call.

- Taking a sabbatical five or six years into a call gives you the opportunity to step back, to reflect on your present call, and to discern whether you're ready and able to stay or to go.

SEVEN THINGS TO KEEP IN MIND WHEN YOU INTERVIEW FOR A NEW CALL

1 Insist on a process steeped in prayer.

Few events in the life of a congregation are charged with as much expectation and possibility as the call process. Anchor the event in prayer. Pray for the congregation. Pray for the call committee. Pray for wisdom and under-

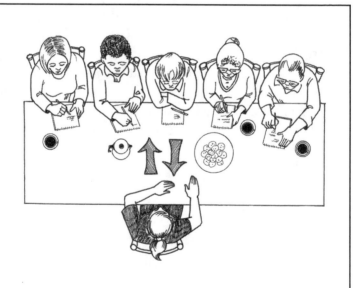

Interviewing for a new call is a two-way affair.
Be ready with thoughtful questions for the call committee
regarding pertinent issues.

standing. Ask the call committee to begin the interview with prayer.

② It's a two-way interview.
You know they'll have questions for you. Come with some questions of your own. For example:

- Tell me about the "golden age" of your congregation.
- If everything goes right, what will this congregation look like in three years?
- Where is God moving in this profile, these newsletters, and these annual reports?
- How is the Holy Spirit agitating in this congregation and in this community?
- What do you want me to ask you and to know about you that I'll never pick up from what you've written about yourselves?
- That's a great question, but I want to ask you first why you ask it.

③ Be yourself—that's who you're going to be anyway.
There's no point trying to impress them with all the things you think they'd like to hear. Know your passions, gifts, interests, growing edges, and limits. That's who you're going to be if they call you.

④ They're not all that interested in what you did in your last congregation.
They're interested in what you can do together in their congregation.

⑤ Turn off your cell phone.
Give the call committee your undivided attention. Then, go ahead and imagine what it would be like to serve with these people. Dream with them about what it would be like to become their pastor.

⑥ Talk about the money.
Someone needs to bring it up. That person might as well be you. Look for an appropriate moment once enough of the interview has elapsed.

⑦ God's Word is always at work, irrespective of you.
God has been here long before you. God will be here long after you. Ministry has been happening. Relax. They don't need a hero or a champion. They want a pastor.

Please Note

- You may discover during the interview that you're still called to the congregation you're serving.

- There's no Nirvana Lutheran Church, and the congregation will discover soon enough that you're not Pastor Perfect.

- The call process is ultimately Spirit territory. Don't be too surprised that it is filled with surprises.

WHAT TO DO WHEN YOU QUESTION WHETHER YOU'RE THE RIGHT PERSON FOR THE CALL YOU'RE IN

❶ Recognize you are in good company.
God's prophets often believed that God made a mistake in calling them to a specific ministry. Self-doubt is a normal experience in all callings, and the pastoral ministry is no exception.

❷ Read your letter of call.
You have a letter of call. This is a request for your services to administer Word and Sacrament, lead the congregation in outreach, and help the congregation grow. More than your self-doubt, the letter of call sets a direction, tone, and parameters to your ministry.

❸ Consider that God may be calling you to something new.
God is ultimately in charge of your ministry, not you. You might feel mismatched, but God wants you to grow in your ministry, gain greater skills, and rely on God in the process.

❹ Continue to minister as if your current call will last forever.
You choose your level of commitment and loyalty in any task you do. Committing yourself again to your call (instead of running from it like Jonah), may offer rich opportunities for you and those to whom you minister.

❺ Remain open to God's shaping.

God is making you to be a person of faith, just like God is doing with every baptized person. Remember, God's power is made perfect in weakness. In times of doubt about your call, you are being stretched beyond your own resources. God promises to be a source of comfort and refuge. God will uphold you.

God is finally in charge of your ministry, not you.
And God is working through you, even when you don't feel it,
so that the congregation grows as well.

⑥ Seek God's vision for ministry in this setting by asking the important questions.

Ask questions in the church council about the mission and ministry of the congregation. Seek to discern what God is calling you to do together in this setting, at this time.

Please Note

- If your situation is untenable, seek out mentors, confessors, and seasoned leaders for counsel. Look for assistance from your bishop.

- The book of Psalms puts our feelings of inadequacy and need into words in light of a faithful God. The prophets also often expressed disappointment with their calls and the people they served. Despite this, they looked for God's help to uphold them in ministry.

HOW TO RETIRE FROM MINISTRY GRACEFULLY

Pastors have the privilege of entering into people's lives with an intimacy available to few other professions. Many pastors become deeply loved and even revered by those they serve. Strong loyalties can also develop. Such attachments make it difficult for many retiring clergy to let go of their call. They can also make it difficult for parishioners to explore God's vision for their mission and ministry with the new pastor. Here are some ways to retire gracefully so you and the congregation can let go without dropping the ball.

❶ Trust God.
Remember that the congregation really belongs to God, not you. Trust that God, even without your help, will be able to support this congregation in ministry. If the congregation is to have a future, there must be a transition in leadership.

❷ Let go, but with explicit and public intentionality.
Tell the congregation publicly that as much as you love them, you will now no longer conduct weddings, baptisms, funerals, pulpit supply, or pastoral counsel for them. Transferring your membership to another parish is appropriate. Tell the congregation you are relinquishing your pastoral duties because you care for the congregation and want it to have a future. You might also mention that you yourself want a future in the freedom of retirement.

❸ Hand over your charge.

A significant indicator of your credibility and success as a pastor is the ability to release your charge into the hands of another. Support your successor both publicly and privately.

A significant indicator of your credibility and success as a pastor is the ability to release your charge into the hands of another.

❹ Honor the office, not your own legacy.
Your successor will not do things exactly as you did them. Even if you disapprove of how your successor does ministry, you can still honor the office of Word and Sacrament ministry that you both share. Speak well of your predecessors and successors.

❺ Pray for the church and your successors by name.
Continue to uphold your former congregation(s) and your successors in prayer.

❻ Take up new or dormant hobbies, volunteer, re-acquaint yourself with your spouse and family.
Busy yourself with things that matter. Don't spend your time trying to find out the latest gossip about your former congregation(s) or successors.

Please Note

- Even if asked to give a eulogy at a funeral because you knew the deceased better than the current pastor, gracefully decline. You, too, did funerals for parishioners you didn't know well when you began your ministry. Let the current pastor find a way to help those who are grieving.

ADMINISTRATIVE STUFF

FIVE TIPS ON HIRING THE RIGHT PERSONNEL TO MAKE A GREAT MINISTRY TEAM

Hiring the right personnel is one of the most important processes in team ministry. These decisions set the parameters for the future stability and growth of your ministry team.

❶ Discern a clear vision for the direction of the ministry team.
A clear vision helps everyone understand the direction of the team and the particular role each person plays.

❷ Develop a specific job description.
Make a realistic, comprehensive, and prioritized list of duties. Clearly identify what you're looking for and what kind of team member you need to enhance the ministry team. Make sure that financial compensation is commensurate to expectations.

❸ Use your networks to find team members.
Ask colleagues for references. Advertise in synod newsletters. Don't limit your networking to church networks, however. There are plenty of Christian people in secular jobs who are very gifted for church work.

❹ Look for initiative and creativity.
A team member will need to respond to unexpected situations and changing needs in the congregation or community. In addition, a creative and entrepreneurial environment will create a context where all team members can thrive.

⑤ In the interview, let the candidate do most of the talking.

Ask four kinds of questions: closed-ended (background), open-ended (based on specific past experience), hypothetical (examples of possible responses or scenarios), and leading (questions that allow the candidate to share her or his vision for the position). Ask all candidates the same questions—questions that clearly and behaviorally demonstrate they have the measurable skills to fulfill the job description and contribute as a member of the ministry team.

*Attempt to detect the creativity level of a candidate
for your ministry staff before offering the job.
A rushed hire is likely to become problematic.*

Please Note

- Take your time and make good decisions. A rushed hire is likely to become problematic if not well-matched with the rest of the team. If a new hire must be let go, expect the team to take more than a year to recover. Replacing a team member can also cost your congregation between one and one half to two and one half times the employee's annual salary.

- If you micromanage, you stifle creativity and will lose good people.

- Once you have your team in place, treat team members well, trust them, and give them the freedom and permission to thrive.

THIRTY SUBJECTS YOU SHOULD NEVER ASK ABOUT WHEN INTERVIEWING FOR NEW STAFF

Getting to know prospective employees within the limitations of an interview can be trying. Resist the temptation, however, to ask personal questions. Asking questions about the following subjects during an interview or on job applications is illegal and simply not worth the risk to you or your congregation.

❶ Marital and family status (for instance, maiden name, spouse's name, spouse's work).

❷ Pregnancy or plans to start a family (for instance, children, number or ages of children, day-care plans).

❸ Age and date of birth.

❹ Sex (only acceptable where Bona Fide Occupational Qualification or BFOQ exists).

❺ Height and weight (only acceptable where BFOQ exists).

❻ Race, color, color of eyes, hair, skin, and complexion.

❼ National origin.

❽ Citizenship (but you may ask if the person is legally permitted to work in the United States).

⑨ Garnishments of wages.

⑩ Credit references, indebtedness (except in cases of job-relatedness and business necessity).

⑪ Arrest record (you can inquire about conviction record, but conviction may not be an absolute bar to employment. You must consider how recent it is and job-relatedness).

⑫ Certain questions about military service (for instance, current military status, branch of service, type of discharge).

⑬ Smoking.

⑭ Person to contact in case of emergency.

⑮ Religion or creed.

⑯ Family members working for organization.

⑰ Sexual orientation.

⑱ Status with regard to public assistance.

⑲ Union membership or sentiments.

⑳ Social Security number.

㉑ Homeowner or renter status.

㉒ Transportation arrangements.

㉓ Past civil lawsuits, judgments against applicant.

㉔ Denied fidelity, surety bond, or government clearance.

㉕ Past workers' compensation claims and injury history.

26 Driver's license (unless necessary for the job).

27 Addictions.

28 Photographs.

29 High school diploma or GED (only acceptable where BFOQ exists).

30 Availability for Saturday or Sunday work (however, you can describe the position and hours and days required, and ask if the person can fulfill these responsibilities).

Please Note

- Consider legal and liability issues of employment with the aid of qualified professionals. Employment laws change over time and may vary according to the size of your church staff. Your local counsel will advise you on the specific laws related to your congregation.

HOW TO EMPOWER YOUR STAFF TO DO GOOD WORK

A congregation's potential to grow is directly related to its staff potential. Empower your staff by establishing common objectives, defining roles, and being specific about each team member's contribution. Communicate openly, honestly, and often.

One way to empower your staff is to use the BEST acronym.

❶ Believe in your staff.
This motivates staff members and releases their potential. By believing in them you engage, equip, and empower staff members to succeed at what they do, and, in turn, your own success increases.

❷ Encourage your staff.
Specific behavioral encouragement helps staff members reach their potential. Let them know their work is important and personally appreciated by you. Catch them doing something good and publicly compliment them, rather than criticizing when they do something wrong. Empower staff members by delegating responsibility to them whenever possible.

❸ Share with your staff.
Create an environment where communication, creativity, and specific expectations are a clear part of the culture. Take time to show sincere interest in each individual, and ask staff members to share their passions, interests, and short and long-range goals.

❹ Trust your staff.

Trust is the glue that holds a staff together. Spend one-on-one time in an atmosphere of honesty and openness. Increase staff members' freedom and responsibility as trust develops. Don't get involved in every detail of their work, but know the range of their responsibilities. Trust them to try out new ideas and encourage them if they fail.

Trust your staff. Trust is the glue that holds a staff together.

Please Note

- Don't underestimate the importance of taking time to have fun together. Lightening the mood in the office increases creativity and boosts productivity. Order pizza on Fridays. Go to a themepark together. Turn the education wing into a miniature golf course and have each staff member responsible for creating a hole. Having fun together regularly will empower your staff to do good work.

FIVE THINGS SENIOR PASTORS CAN DO TO ENDEAR THEMSELVES TO THEIR STAFF

Senior pastors and staff members exist in a symbiotic relationship: The primary duty of staff members is to make the senior pastor look good. The primary duty of senior pastors is to make staff members look good. As long as everyone does his or her duty, everyone looks good.

1 Give credit where due.
Nothing ruins morale more quickly than the senior pastor taking credit for an idea, program, or other success that actually came from a staff member. Always give credit to the staff member who carried out the idea, even if it was your idea. Give extra credit if it really was the staff member's idea.

2 Respect professional boundaries.
If you've hired a youth director, let the youth director do youth ministry. Butt out unless asked. Same for letting the minister of music do music, and the visitation pastor do visitation. You hired these people because they were experts. Even if you did these things well before they were hired, it's someone else's job now.

3 Provide real support, not just pep talks.
If a staff member expresses concern that a program or ministry is not going well, he or she probably needs specific suggestions on how to fix the problem, not just a pat on the back and a "Go get 'em, tiger," speech.

④ Communicate.

Communication is a two-way street. You have to listen as well as talk. Keep your staff members in the loop and make sure they know what you are up to at all times. Expect that they will not surprise you, but that they will likewise keep you informed.

⑤ Say "Thank you."

Above all, express appreciation for the work of your staff, and make sure the congregation regularly hears you doing so. Demonstrating appreciation with a gift, a bonus, a salary increase, or other benefits is also highly motivating.

A less-popular method of endearing one's self to your staff may involve self-deprecating humor.

HOW TO RUN A STAFF MEETING

Nearly every congregation has a staff of some sort, even if it consists of only two people. Administrative assistants, youth directors, custodians, organists, and choir directors, whether they are volunteers or in paid positions, count as staff. Your staff members probably do not work together in the same office space 40 hours a week, which makes it critical they meet regularly at an appointed time to coordinate ministry efforts. An efficient staff meeting will include at least five elements.

❶ Begin with prayer.
Above all, staff members are people. They have families, joys, sorrows, health concerns, and other personal issues. Sharing these is a way of providing support and pastoral care for those who are ministering to others. Lifting these concerns in prayer deepens the staff's commitment to one another and builds spiritual strength.

❷ Discuss any immediate concerns.
Deal immediately with concerns staff members have alerted you to prior to the meeting, or concerns staff members bring with them. These include questions, interpersonal conflicts, or other matters of concern. Staff members will think about these things—rather than any other agenda items—until they are resolved, so address them right away.

❸ Look at the calendar.
Review the congregation's calendar for the upcoming several weeks to help everyone coordinate efforts and avoid major conflicts. The secretary or other "keeper" of the calendar can read through items day by day. Other

staff members can add details to be included in bulletins, newsletters, or other publicity.

❹ **Consider issues related to long-term projects.**
Add calendar items beyond the next several weeks with details to follow. Big events or programs in the planning stages can be discussed, ideas and suggestions contributed, and the like. For example, November meetings should involve discussions of Lent and Easter plans.

Good staff coordination depends upon regular calendar maintenance. Make sure to cover important events to avoid being caught by surprise.

January meetings should involve plans for vacation Bible school and summer camps.

⑤ Be proactive.
Don't fall into the trap of only being driven by the calendar or just reacting to current problems. Spend a few minutes at the end of each staff meeting brainstorming new approaches, new programs, or new ways of doing ministry. Encourage staff members to bring their ideas and add to and expand on the dreams of others.

HOW TO FIRE SOMEONE WHEN YOU REALLY HAVE TO

Firing someone doesn't feel good, but sometimes for the good of the congregation you have to. When that time comes, it's important to act with both sensitivity and knowledge of good employment practice.

1 Work with a personnel committee.
A personnel committee can help write job descriptions, handle difficulties, review performances, and hire and fire employees.

2 Have written job descriptions in place.
Everyone—including important volunteers—should have written job descriptions spelling out expectations and accountability. Refer to these documents whenever there are difficulties.

3 When there's difficulty, prepare prayerfully for the first meeting.
Call a meeting with the personnel committee to prepare for the first meeting with the employee. Pray and think carefully together.

4 Agree on what needs to change.
Meet with the employee and communicate clearly, and in writing, the actions and words that are creating problems. Give the employee every reasonable chance and enough time to improve. Involve him or her in coming to a change you all find workable.

⑤ Develop an action plan.
If there is no improvement, call a second meeting to develop an action plan and timeline with the employee. Make sure that the employee has a copy of the plan and understands and agrees to the plan. The expectations should be realistic, very clear, measurable, and specific.

⑥ End the person's employment if the plan isn't followed.
If the employee does not follow the action plan and meet the deadlines, proceed to end employment. It may be appropriate to give the employee an opportunity to resign. Make sure one or two others can be present for the meeting. Bring all your documentation, including a written record of progress or lack of it. Do not waver or sound "iffy," but be respectful if the person gets emotional and give him or her time to regain self-control.

⑦ Evaluate the experience and be respectful of reactions.
Evaluate with your leaders what you might learn from this experience. Be sensitive and respectful about differences of opinion and differing reactions. If there are negative reactions within the congregation, overcome evil with good. Whenever possible, do not keep secrets but communicate the problems and the process.

Please Note
- Written documentation is very important.
- If there is any reason to suspect the employee may become violent during the final meeting, notify a professional (security agent or local police officer) ahead of time or have her or him close by.

- When an employee moves to litigation, it is often because the process of termination was not handled properly and respectfully, and the employee seeks revenge or due process.

- The process for terminating the call of any rostered leader in the Evangelical Lutheran Church in America (ELCA) requires consulting with the synod bishop and following the process spelled out in the constitution of the synod and the ELCA.

HOW TO GET THE BEST OUT OF THE CHURCH ADMINISTRATIVE ASSISTANT

Nearly every congregation today has someone serving in the administrative assistant role. This person may be a full time professional or a volunteer serving a few hours a week. In any case, the pastor can realize the greatest benefit from such a person by making him or her a partner or team member rather than a lackey or servant.

❶ Anticipate.
Try to look ahead and anticipate tasks that need to be accomplished. Avoid creating a crisis by waiting until the last minute with tasks that need to be completed. Establish a work routine that allows the administrative assistant to develop clear expectations about what will need to be done and when.

❷ Communicate.
Establish clear policies and general procedures, and make these explicitly clear to the administrative assistant. Do not force the assistant to read your mind or guess your intentions in day-to-day situations. Make your priorities clearly understood.

❸ Empower.
Don't second-guess decisions made in your absence. Give your administrative assistant confidence that when he or she must react to a situation for which there are no clear policies in place, you will stand by that decision and be

supportive, trusting that it was the best possible decision at the time.

❹ Delegate.
Everyone does not go about a task in the same way, but the end result may be equally successful. Don't micromanage. Allow the administrative assistant the latitude necessary to complete tasks assigned. Clearly communicate what is expected and when it must be completed, then get out of the way.

Avoid creating a crisis. Don't wait until the last minute with tasks that need to be completed.

⑤ Listen.

Let your administrative assistant know you are willing to hear concerns or problems that make it difficult for him or her to do the job effectively—even when the problem is you! Work together to solve problems and address concerns.

⑥ Train.

Most people find fulfillment in developing new skills and enhancing old ones to become better and more professional at what they do. Offer time and money for continuing education, particularly when a new piece of equipment or new computer software is introduced.

⑦ Appreciate.

Most likely your administrative assistant isn't in this work for the huge salary. Regular use of the phrase "thank you" and public expressions of appreciation before the gathered congregation will go a long way toward making the job fulfilling and satisfying.

HOW TO RELATE EFFECTIVELY TO A SENIOR COLLEAGUE

To develop the best working relationship, it's important to understand your senior colleague's personality traits, leadership style, and supervisory approach. Give your senior colleague the confidence that you are a team player and can be depended on to make his or her job easier. Let your senior colleague know you understand his or her goals and that you know your part in accomplishing those goals.

1 Know your job inside and out.

If you are faced with something new, put in the necessary time on your own to figure things out. Develop a menu of options, and then decide together on the best course of action.

2 Always publicly support your senior colleague.

While there's always room for private conversation about issues, it's important for the congregation to know that nothing can come between you and your senior colleague.

3 Communicate openly and often.

Make sure your senior colleague knows what you're thinking and planning.

4 Under-promise and over-deliver.

Get your work done when you said you would—without exception. And then do everything you do with excellence.

HOW TO RELATE EFFECTIVELY TO A JUNIOR COLLEAGUE

As a supervisor, you play an important role in the development of a junior colleague. You bring a wide range of life and work experiences, and you can act as an important source of advice and information. Always look for ways to train and develop a junior colleague's skills to improve his or her chances of success.

❶ Offer advice judiciously.
Encourage your junior colleague to solve his or her own problems, while recognizing that occasionally you may be able to provide a helpful second opinion or different perspective. You can be a mentor as your junior colleague grows and gains new skills and confidence. Establish a relationship of trust, and never be condescending in giving advice.

❷ Provide plenty of access.
The most important thing you can give your junior colleague is access to your time. Take time together, but don't do all the talking. Always seek to give more than you receive. Make this a priority each week.

❸ Advocate on behalf of your junior colleague.
Be an advocate for your junior colleague to get him or her the recognition he or she deserves. Create opportunities that help build self-confidence and encourage professional advancement. Be a coach day to day, and a cheerleader long-term. Help your junior colleague be the best in everything he or she does.

FIVE COMMON PITFALLS SOLO PASTORS FALL INTO AND HOW TO AVOID THEM

It is easy for solo pastors to feel the weight of responsibility for the congregation, its leaders, and its members. Take your call seriously, while keeping your eyes open for some of the common pitfalls you may encounter.

① Boredom with preaching.
It's not just the people in the pew who can get tired of the pastor's preaching. You might be bored, too. Preaching 50-plus sermons a year can do it. Add opportunities for creative approaches to preaching. Consider skits involving others to share the gospel message.

② It's my church.
Develop a daily ritual to remind yourself that Christ's church does not belong to any human being, either lay or clergy. This may be a repetitive prayer or a physical reminder, such as a plaque or Bible verse. This will help you center yourself when things don't go as you hope they will.

③ The vision is mine.
People will look to the pastor to create and communicate the vision for the church. This is based on an old model of ministry that actually undermines our Lutheran theology. Educate leaders to understand that the vision for ministry is owned by the corporate body and fueled by the power of the Holy Spirit.

❹ They need me.

You may feel that it is appropriate to drop whatever you are doing and run when someone contacts you. When contacted for assistance, first determine if it is a life-and-death situation. If it is not, it may not require immediate attention. It is okay to set boundaries on your work and personal time.

If you're bored with your preaching, there's a good chance others are too.

⑤ I'm all alone.

As a solo pastor, you may feel like you are going it alone. Maintain connections with other pastors in the conference and synod. Participate in colleague groups to learn from and support each other.

Please Note

- These pitfalls may also trip up pastors serving with other staff members. Pay attention to your leadership style and what it communicates to your lay leaders and to the congregation.

- The temptation to skip days off may be greater for solo pastors. If an emergency prevents you from taking a day off, make it up elsewhere. Since you are on call 24/7, you need time off. Take it.

TEN TIPS FOR BUILDING EFFECTIVE PASTORAL RELATIONSHIPS IN A CONGREGATION

Effective pastoral relationships don't develop all at once. They are built over time with individuals, groups, and the congregation as a whole. Remember to love and respect your people and their traditions, congregational property, your staff and coworkers, and the gospel and its power. Here are 10 tips:

❶ **Appreciated people rarely complain.**
Practice the spiritual gifts of hospitality and gratitude. And remember, for every complaint, there are probably two or three more who feel the same—and 50 who don't.

❷ **Spend a year getting to know the traditions of the congregation.**
If you are in a new call, listen and learn before making changes. Then communicate and educate about variations you want to make. Avoid making quick movements or sharp sounds, as many members may be skittish.

❸ **Involve a group of people.**
When making changes in worship styles, educational adventures, or new organizational styles, involve a task force or committee in the decision-making process. Communicate well and take action one step at a time. (See number 2 again.)

❹ Look for spiritual and relational gifts in all ages.
Some children can read well. Others are accomplished
musicians. Some adults like to light candles. Young
people can be greeters. Infants often "cry out" in tongues
during worship and should be recognized.

❺ Think outside the doors.
Not all "ministry" happens within the walls of the
church building. Consider modeling good stewardship
by "tithing" your time, giving 10 percent to the greater
church or to the community.

*Show up at football games,
band concerts, and fund-
raisers—uninvited.*

⑥ **Learn to be good at remembering names.**
Using a person's name informally or during the Eucharist shows respect and builds community. Avoid calling someone by the wrong name, as this can cause tribulation and occasional teeth gnashing.

⑦ **Show genuine interest, whenever possible.**
Make it part of your weekly schedule to attend your flock's community activities. Show up at football games, band concerts, and fund-raisers—uninvited.

⑧ **Honor your days off.**
Take vacations and use all your continuing education time and funds. This will make you a better pastor and a good role model for your congregation and may yield greater dividends in the future.

⑨ **Surround yourself with support.**
You don't have a corner on all the spiritual gifts. You may, in fact, be possessed of only a few. Know your own gifts and deficits. Know when to defer to a greater authority: a homeless shelter, a women's resource center, a hospital, and a mental health counselor. This helps to preserve your strength and increase your effectiveness.

⑩ **Love your family.**
Pay attention to them and don't assume they will participate in the life of the church the way "everyone" expects. Ask them to serve just as you would ask anyone else, but avoid overburdening them just because they're close at hand.

FOUR UNLIKELY LEADERS IN THE BIBLE AND WHAT YOU CAN LEARN FROM THEM

Actually, all the leaders of God's people in the Bible were unlikely. Moses was an escaped slave and a murderer. Peter was a lowly fisherman who denied Jesus. Mary was pregnant out of wedlock. Jeremiah was a teenager. They were all sinners with low potential, every last one.

❶ Paul.

Paul was born Saul, "of the tribe of Benjamin, a Hebrew born of Hebrews; as to the law, a Pharisee; as to zeal, a persecutor of the church" (Philippians 3:5-6). But the Lord called Paul and sent him to be an apostle to the Gentiles (Galatians 2:8). He was the last person any human would have imagined as a leader in the church, but he was the one God chose. From Paul's story, we learn that the basic qualification a person needs to be a Christian leader is to be forgiven. We also learn that our call is to preach "Christ crucified" (1 Corinthians 1:23)—we do not proclaim the hidden majesty of God, but the power of God hidden in the lowly criminal crucified for us.

❷ David.

David was the youngest son of Jesse. God sent the prophet Samuel to anoint one of Jesse's sons as the new king of Israel. Samuel looked at David's older, stronger, better-looking brothers and figured one of them would be the new king. Jesse didn't even show David to Samuel! But God had chosen David, because God does not look on outward appearance, but "looks on the heart"

(1 Samuel 16:7). David's story teaches us not to judge the ability of others to lead in the church based on their "profile." From his later life and his adultery with Bathsheba and his murder of Bathsheba's husband, we also learn that leaders remain sinners after they are called. And leaders always need forgiveness.

❸ and ❹ Shiphrah and Puah.
When God's people were enslaved in Egypt, Pharaoh ordered that all newborn Hebrew boys be killed. But

God worked through Shiphrah and Puah, two slave midwives.

Shiphrah and Puah, two slave midwives, revered God more than they feared Pharaoh, so they disobeyed. Shiphrah and Puah took leadership and responsibility. In the ancient world, it was hard to find someone lower on the social food chain than slave midwives, but they took the first steps that eventually led to the Exodus. Shiphrah and Puah teach us God can work through anyone.

HOW TO RELEASE YOUR CONGREGATION'S ABILITY TO DEVELOP A VISION FOR MINISTRY

Pastors don't develop the vision for a congregation's ministry. In fact, no solitary person develops it, and personal agendas should be avoided during the vision process. It is the work of the congregation and its leaders, including the pastor, to discern God's vision for your shared ministry. Seek the inspiration of the Holy Spirit as you work to discover this vision.

❶ Root the process in prayer.
Encourage everyone to engage in both individual and corporate prayer. Seek the guidance of the Holy Spirit throughout your vision process.

❷ Study the Bible for insights.
Look for biblical vision statements. Explore Jesus' vision for ministry. Read and discuss the book of Acts. Probe the early church's vision for ministry, and study how it changed over time.

❸ Look outward.
Study your community to determine whether it has changed since your congregation started. List the assets and needs of your community. Seek input from community members.

❹ Look inward.

Study your congregation to determine whether it has changed since it started. List the assets and needs of the congregation. Seek input from members.

❺ Compare the outward and inward assets and needs.

Look for differences and similarities. Explore new ways your congregation can use its assets and interact with the community.

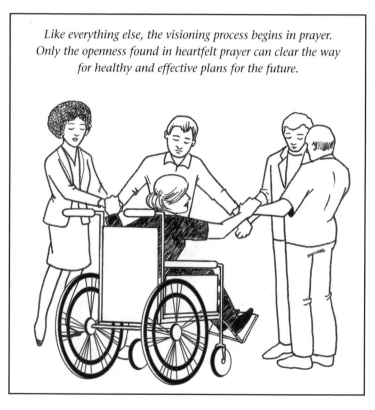

Like everything else, the visioning process begins in prayer. Only the openness found in heartfelt prayer can clear the way for healthy and effective plans for the future.

⑥ Brainstorm words and ideas for the vision.
Brainstorming thoughts about your congregation's future may create new possibilities for ministry in your community. Some people avoid change and may fight new ideas that arise from a brainstorming process. Stay rooted in prayer and Scripture.

⑦ Write the vision down on paper, then post it so everyone can see.
Keep it short so that you will remember it. Have the congregation vote on the new vision statement. Publish it and refer to it when creating new ministries.

Please Note

- Using a process to discover God's vision for your congregation can be risky. You won't know in advance what that vision might be. The unknown scares some people, who typically react against it with vigor and determination. Communicate clearly and openly, but be ready for resistance.

- Visions for ministry should change when there are changes in your congregation or community. Be sure to review your vision every three years to ensure adherence.

HOW TO DELEGATE

Pastors have many demands upon their time, so it's important to determine the best use of your time. This is where
delegation is helpful.

1 Identify your pastoral responsibilities.
List the responsibilities only you can do. Be honest with
yourself.

2 Review your weekly schedule.
List the tasks that currently consume your time.

3 Compare your lists.
Is your weekly schedule filled with duties that others can
perform? For example, if you have a secretary, copying
the weekly bulletins may not be the best use of your time.

4 Consider the gifts of others.
Before delegating to other people, consider their gifts and
abilities. When uncertain, ask them.

5 Make the request.
Ask someone else to complete duties that do not require
your personal attention. This gets easier with time and
practice.

6 Follow through.
Trust that the person to whom you have delegated will
perform the assigned task. It is acceptable to ask about
the outcome.

Please Note

- Church culture often encourages pastors to over-function and attempt to do everything themselves. Delegating can help prevent feelings of fatigue and burnout.

- Conversely, avoid over-delegating. Assume responsibility for your duties daily to avoid laziness and sloth.

Church culture often encourages pastors to over-function and to do everything themselves. Delegating tasks others are well-equipped to perform can mitigate burnout and expand your ministry.

HOW TO ENABLE YOUR CONGREGATION TO LIVE AS THE PRIESTHOOD OF ALL BELIEVERS

Lutherans adhere to a doctrine called "the priesthood of all believers," but don't assume everyone remembers what this means from their days in confirmation. Anticipate some discomfort with the concept because it implies a daily responsibility for Christian living. Proceed anyway.

❶ Familiarize your congregation with Martin Luther's interpretation of this concept.
Luther believed the church was founded on Christ's priesthood and that each Christian had priestly duties in both the church and the world. These duties include praying for each other, sharing God's Word by talking about the life of faith, and forgiving one another.

❷ Preach the biblical views of priesthood.
Look for examples of how God calls us to be members of the priesthood of all believers. Read and reflect on 1 Peter 2:9-10.

❸ Model it.
Encourage members of your congregation to reflect on how they pray for each other by telling them how you do it. Be transparent about your own priesthood and daily struggles. Discuss how they currently share their faith stories with others. How do they practice forgiveness? How can they expand on faith activities they already engage in?

4 Celebrate the daily ministries of your members in public worship.

This might be done through a sermon or a special worship service. For instance, Reformation Sunday is a good time to lift up the priesthood of all believers with anecdotes and everyday examples.

5 Pray for your members' ministry and mission.

This is the most obvious, but it can be the easiest step to overlook. Pray that members of the congregation will come to a deeper understanding of what it means to be "priests" in daily living.

Create opportunities to celebrate the daily ministries of your members.

Please Note

- If a pastor claims to be the absolute religious authority in the local congregation, this may undermine the priesthood of all believers. Lay people may begin to feel disempowered.

- People who are already overwhelmed by demands in their daily lives may hear the call to be a priest as one more burden on their schedules. Explain that this is not a burden, but something for which they are empowered by the Holy Spirit.

HOW TO PARTICIPATE IN A COMMITTEE MEETING WITHOUT HAVING TO BE IN CHARGE

When it comes to committee or team meetings, though it might be easier to simply charge ahead, the purpose of a committee structure in a congregation is to enable lay members to assume responsibility for and ownership of ministry decisions. It is vital that group members leave the meeting feeling as though they have made important decisions, and not that you have dictated your wishes to them.

❶ Hold a conversation with the chairperson prior to the meeting and agree on what the agenda should include.
Negotiate agenda items, even if this means including some that are unnecessary or less important, in your view, than the items you suggest. Share the agenda with all committee members prior to the meeting, through mail or e-mail.

❷ Allow the chairperson to run the agenda.
This may require some patience and restraint because you may actually be more skilled at running a meeting than the designated chairperson. But the best way to avoid being in charge is to not be the designated leader.

❸ Offer to take notes. Occasionally.
Most people hate being the secretary of a meeting, maintaining the minutes, or preparing the committee report, but you may have far more ability to shape the official

outcome of a meeting by describing what happened than by making things happen. Just don't make a habit of it.

❹ **Influence the meeting primarily by serving as the source of information.**
Members of a committee, team, or task group will often turn to you because you naturally have more information and day-to-day experience with church matters than they. Share what you know, as appropriate, without using information to dominate or to squelch others' ideas.

❺ **Accept and support the outcome, even if it wasn't the decision you had hoped for.**
If the course of action decided upon does not yield the desired result, the matter can almost always be reconsidered at a later meeting.

HOW TO TAKE CHARGE OF A COMMITTEE MEETING WHEN IT GETS OFF TRACK

Considerable sensitivity and aplomb is required when determining whether a committee or other task group has lost its way. Sometimes an off-task conversation or some frivolous banter is just what the group members need to build trust with one another and enjoy themselves. However, if the meeting really has gone astray, try these tactics:

When a committee reaches an impasse, it is appropriate for you, as a pastor, to suggest the group members take a break and return to the subject when they can devote themselves to it more fully.

❶ Ask a question.
Say something like, "Remind me, what did we decide on that last issue?" It may serve to remind others that they hadn't yet reached a decision before getting sidetracked.

❷ Act as a gatekeeper.
Gain the group's attention and invite someone who is waiting to get back on track to speak: "Julie, what were you thinking about our fall program plans?"

❸ Make a suggestion.
To return the focus to the task at hand, suggest an idea that will move the task forward: "Getting back to what Tom suggested earlier, what about adding a coffee bar to the pastors' lounge?"

❹ Take a break.
If all else fails, suggest taking a break and coming back when people are ready to give attention to the task. This may be in 10 minutes, or perhaps next month. Be careful not to do this when you're the only one who needs a break.

HOW TO SUPPORT AND EMPOWER THE CHURCH COUNCIL WITHOUT BECOMING A DICTATOR OR A WALLFLOWER

Pastors and congregation councils need to support and empower one another, but often the pastor-council relationship is antagonistic. This sort of adversarial relationship is quite unhealthy for the pastor, as well as for the congregation. Therefore, pastors and lay leaders need to work toward a relationship of mutual respect and support. Here's how you can support the council.

❶ Collaborate on a thorough plan well in advance of council meetings.
Meet with the council president to agree on a detailed agenda prior to each meeting, so that council members can receive an agenda well enough in advance to come prepared for the meeting and important issues are discussed in a timely manner.

❷ Prepare the members by keeping them well-informed.
See to it that all council members are supplied with up-to-date copies of the constitution, bylaws, and continuing resolutions of the congregation, and that they have full access to timely financial reports.

❸ Train the leadership fully, then expect their best.
Provide council members with adequate training for their
jobs with congregational resources, synod workshops,
and other educational opportunities.

❹ Apprise council members of your team's goings-on.
Keep council members aware of your professional activities and those of other staff members so that they can
respond knowledgeably if questioned about these.

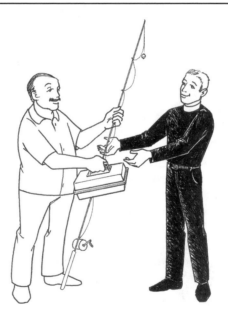

Support and empower the church council. Council members,
in turn, can support a pastor and staff by insisting that
days off and vacations are taken and that attention is given
to self and family care.

⑤ Drive gently toward consensus and a conclusion.
Allow the council to deliberate and decide issues with
complete information, but without coercion or pressure.
People tend to appreciate closure while they may not
react well to interminable indecision.

⑥ Support the council's work publicly.
Stand by and support council decisions, even if you don't
fully agree with them.

**⑦ Pray for your council and the leadership they provide
to the congregation.**
Help them to come to their task prayerfully by arranging
for meetings to include devotions and study time.

HOW TO SURVIVE AN ANNUAL MEETING

The annual meeting of the congregation is typically the highest decision-making body in the congregation, with complete authority over the ministry, priorities, property, staff, budget, and leadership of the congregation. Consequently, these meetings can become a source of stress for clergy. To minimize this stress, follow these steps:

1 Prepare for any reasonable questions, complaints, or issues that might arise.
Anticipate which topics may be brought up from the floor, and consider in advance how they can be addressed. Keep on the lookout starting a couple of months ahead of time. Annual meetings are not a good time for surprises.

2 Establish a detailed agenda.
Include all necessary and desired items on the prepared agenda. Formally defer less pressing "ad hoc" items to a future meeting or to action by the council when leaders are better prepared to deal with them.

3 Begin the meeting with prayer.

4 Dispense with weighty matters up front.
Get any difficult business taken care of right away. Leave time for celebration and fellowship toward the end of the meeting when the mood lightens.

⑤ Move the meeting along.

Consult with the congregational president (usually the meeting's chairperson) to ensure he or she will keep the meeting moving at a brisk pace through the agenda. No one appreciates a meeting that drags on. Issues requiring lengthy deliberation should go through a committee process before coming to the whole congregation.

Keep things moving along at the annual meeting so people's minds don't wander.

⑥ Evaluate the process and outcomes.
After the meeting, consider what you can learn from the experience about the congregational mood, issues to be addressed in the coming year, and how to be better prepared next time.

Please Note

- Keeping the atmosphere as lighthearted as possible will help prevent feelings of being overwhelmed and expedite the process. Consider having the council wear loud clothes or false moustaches, or both, should the mood permit.

TEN THINGS ABOUT PARISH MINISTRY THEY DIDN'T TEACH YOU IN SEMINARY

❶ God was present and at work in the congregation before you arrived.

Instead of devaluing or discounting the work that the congregation and your predecessors have done, honor these and build on them. Extending previous visions can facilitate whatever new one God has under your leadership.

❷ The congregation doesn't care how things were done in your last call.

You will be tempted to recreate your successes in each place you serve. Many ideas may transfer—if they are presented as new possibilities and allowed to grow in unique ways within each setting. Avoid foisting. Foisting is not good pastoral leadership.

❸ The congregation needs a pastor more than it needs another member.

You may be reluctant to relinquish the joy of your individual identity, but your primary role within the congregation is connected to the pastoral office. Graceful acceptance of this office will allow you to develop fulfilling pastoral relationships.

4 The congregation will be able to find another pastor, but your spouse and/or family cannot find a replacement so easily.

Good stewardship of your family relationships will enhance your ministry in a way that allows it to endure long-term.

Your congregation may need a cheerleader to cheer everyone on.

5 Sometimes a congregation needs a cheerleader more than a prophet, a preacher, or a priest.
A "cheerleader" names a goal, focuses everyone's attention on accomplishing it, and leads the celebration when the goal is met. Many congregations are capable of accomplishing great things if someone simply cheers them on.

6 Your job is not to create the perfect Lutheran congregation. Such does not exist.
In seminary you were appropriately taught the Lutheran confessions and denominational history. But remember, each congregation is a rich mix of many influences. Like a spouse, a congregation cannot be molded into perfection so much as walked with faithfully.

7 You do not have to be the most knowledgeable person in every area of the congregation's ministry, tempting though this may be.
Leading is done best by knowing whom to follow in the various aspects of a congregation's ministry. Always allow and appreciate the expertise of others.

8 "Here I stand" is not always the best stance for pastors.
It worked for Martin Luther, but context is everything. Flexibility and a broad vision of God's work in the world can allow you to bring a grace-filled approach to ministry. Also consider historical, biblical, confessional, and theological thinking as these apply to the context of the congregation.

⑨ Grace applies to pastors too.
You are called to lead faithfully, not perfectly or tirelessly. God's unqualified love allows you to admit mistakes and also rest when needed. Authenticity involves recognizing your limitations.

⑩ Business and ministry concerns are not opposed to one another.
Good congregational leadership includes upholding good business practice while striving for effective ministry. Become familiar with sound business skills and practices, then lead the council and congregation to see that these are always aimed at the primary goal of doing ministry.

HOW TO READ A CONGREGATIONAL FINANCIAL STATEMENT (AND WHY IT'S IMPORTANT)

A congregational financial statement can help you learn a lot about a congregation and its mission. This is especially important to do when considering a call to a particular congregation.

❶ Look at expenses.

On the spending side, you'll find plenty of unglamorous line items (such as toilet paper and light bulbs) that may not seem mission-driven at all. But if the congregation's rest rooms lacked light and toilet paper, would that be hospitable to newcomers hungering for the gospel? The same goes for heat.

❷ Look at benevolence.

What does the congregation support with its dollars? From these line items, you can get a sense of the congregation's identity. If you are a pastor of this congregation, do these items reflect the values and ministry happening here? If not, what can be done to change this?

❸ Look at income.

There may be some surprising things here, like rent paid by the child-care center or a Tuesday night Alcoholics Anonymous group, but the bulk of the congregation's income will be from member giving. If members make an annual commitment for their giving, there may be a category for pledges. Loose change, meaning money that just showed up outside of anything that was pledged, may also be included.

❹ Look at the bottom line.
The bottom line is, "Is the congregation solvent?" If the answer is "no," this may be intentional. Some congregations create what they call "mission-driven" or "growth" budgets, which means they are going to deliberately overspend to attract new members (and more income) with new programs and staff. Sometimes this is just the thing, but this can't go on year after year unless they have a track record to prove they can pull it off. If the answer is "yes," look for a vision that's driving the congregation's financial life. It costs money to do ministry. Is the congregation living on its endowment or slowly shriveling up? Is it leaning into its future? Is it putting its money where its mouth is?

Please Note

- Someone in a congregation may say the amount in the "staff salaries" line item is too high. There you are in a congregational meeting suddenly having a public conversation about something that most of us talk about behind closed doors with only our bosses in the room. Don't let this distract you. While it's possible the staff is overpaid, this is rare.

- Notice the ebbs and flows in member giving. Summer is often sparse. December is often heavy. The more even the giving, the better the cash flow, since bill-paying generally requires a more steady supply.

HOW TO MANAGE YOUR CALENDAR

Whether you're the senior pastor of a mega-church in Minnesota or a pastoral intern at a rural congregation in West Virginia, you have 168 hours each week at your personal discretion. How you spend those hours makes all the difference.

❶ Identify how you spend your time.
Keep a ministry activity log for one week, then decide which tasks can be delegated to a staff member, an administrative assistant, or a ministry team.

❷ Make a list of everything you need to do in the next day, week, and month.
Realistically determine the amount of time each task will take, including transportation time and preparation. Differentiate between fixed commitments and flexible commitments, and assign appropriate priorities as you schedule your time. If your congregation council establishes annual goals, those goals should guide your priorities.

❸ Set future priorities.
Beyond the next month, carefully consider which tasks simply cannot wait and those that may be optional. Create a list of priorities that includes how much time you'll spend on each item. Prioritize the tasks in order of importance and urgency. Set personal boundaries, and decide what you can and cannot do.

4 Avoid perfectionism. It leads to burnout.
Set realistic goals and strive to do what you do with excellence, but decide which tasks need less than perfection.

5 Conquer the clutter.
Change habits that lead to messes and disorganization. Be aware of how your time is spent most effectively.

Please Note

- Say "no" to requests for your time if they only add extra stress to your life without moving you or your ministry forward. You simply can't do everything you'd like to do. Talk with trusted mentors to find out how they manage their time and what they say "no" to.

- Get adequate sleep. The more demands you make on yourself, the more sleep you need.

HOW TO CARVE OUT TIME FOR SERMON PREPARATION

Making time for sermon preparation is easy—all you have to do is have a predictable schedule in a profession where unpredictability is the order of the day. The key to sermon preparation is to have a routine, even though some weeks that routine will fall into hopeless disarray. (If this sounds like a lot of work, consider the importance of the task.) Your routine might look something like this:

❶ Make any preparation time you spend in your church office officially sacrosanct.
Black it out on your calendar and the church calendar. Make a sign that reads "Sermon Preparation in Progress: Do Not Disturb" and hang it on your door. Allow no exceptions.

❷ Spend some time very early in the week with the passage you're preaching on.
Read it in several translations. Study a commentary or two. If you're one of "those" preachers, translate it from the original language as part of your regular discipline.

❸ Gather with colleagues in a text study.
Nothing gets the homiletical juices flowing faster than stimulating conversation, especially if undertaken with those whose opinions differ widely. Besides, you can steal a good example or two.

❹ Pray through the passage and then let it ruminate.
Read another commentary or two. Reread the text several times, looking for something you haven't seen before.

⑤ Make an outline.

Even if you're an excellent extemporaneous speaker, making an outline will serve to organize your thoughts and boost your delivery.

⑥ Rewrite and practice the delivery.

Preach into a tape recorder, then listen to your delivery to identify weak spots or phrases you'd like to emphasize. If you dare, practice preaching in a mirror to get those killer gestures down pat.

Join a text study group. Nothing gets the homiletical juices flowing faster than stimulating conversation.

HOW TO LEAD A RETREAT

When done correctly, retreats are a wonderful way to enhance discipleship and community among the people of the congregation.

❶ Determine the purpose of the retreat, if you must.
A retreat should enhance and lift up the mission and vision of the congregation in a more intimate and community-related fashion. Possible purposes include visioning by the leadership team, Sunday school fellowship, confirmation instruction, or women's or men's groups. But really, you don't need much of a reason to take a retreat.

❷ Clearly define the audience.
The target audience will determine the type, length, and setting of the retreat. Younger disciples require much exercise. Older disciples require much coffee and doughnuts.

❸ Atmosphere is important.
Your audience and retreat topic define the atmosphere. Possible atmospheres include fun, family-oriented, somber, prayerful, or challenging. For overnight retreats, consider handing out ear plugs in cases where snoring may occur.

❹ Determine the type of material to be covered.
Purchase or create programming that is appropriate for the age, audience, topic, atmosphere, and location. This is the crux of a well-done retreat. Spend a good deal of time on this step. Ask colleagues or parishioners about material they have used in the past, and what was helpful

or unhelpful about it. Check with synod resource centers for new and well-received programs.

⑤ Create a schedule and follow it.
Outline a schedule that allows adequate time to cover the material and provides for fun, fellowship, and needed rest. Don't over-schedule, especially if children, elderly people, or families will be involved. Give each person a copy of the schedule and post it around the retreat location.

Don't over-schedule a retreat. Allow time for fun, fellowship, and needed rest.

⑥ Reserve a location well in advance.
If you have not previously visited the location, try to do so prior to making a reservation if distance allows. Determine whether adequate space is available for programming. Consider space for bad weather, games, small groups, or meals.

⑦ Recruit plenty of volunteers.
Retreats involve a great deal of work. Do not attempt to pull off a retreat as a "Lone Ranger." Clearly define your expectations. If possible, as a congregation, give volunteers financial assistance with any cost involved in attending the retreat.

⑧ Determine a reasonable cost.
Based on materials, travel, room and board, and meeting space cost, determine how much each individual or family will need to pay to cover the cost of the retreat.

⑨ Acquaint yourself with the material.
Take time in advance to learn and practice all program material. A successful retreat leader is well-versed in the topic for the retreat. Do not wait until you arrive on-site to prepare.

⑩ Make a supply list.
After you have studied the material, make a list of supplies you will need for games, activities, small groups, refreshments, and meetings. Purchase list items prior to arriving at the location. Hang on to your receipts.

⑪ Pull it all together.
Thoughtfully and intentionally pull together all of the above steps for a wonderful and life-changing retreat. If

you've done your work well to this point, a good retreat is virtually guaranteed.

⑫ Evaluate the retreat one week hence.
Create an evaluation form for participants to complete at the end of the retreat, then review feedback with your volunteers a week later.

Please Note

- Learning the material is the highest priority. Don't get bogged down by the "busy work" and allow this step to fall by the wayside.

- The location of the retreat may not be suitable for running out for supplies at the last minute.

- Purchase supplies only after the number of registrations is fairly firm. This will keep you from over- or under-purchasing. Turn in all your receipts for reimbursement.

PASTORAL STUFF

LUTHER'S FIVE BIGGEST PASTORAL DILEMMAS AND HOW HE HANDLED THEM

❶ To wed or not.
Martin Luther had argued for releasing monks and nuns from their vows and for the marriage of priests. Some nuns heard Luther's message and sneaked away from their abbey. They wanted Luther to find husbands for them, which he was able to do for all but one. He followed through and gave up the celibate life to marry the former nun, Katharina von Bora.

❷ The Peasants' War.
In 1525, the peasants of southern Germany revolted violently. They thought they had found permission for their fight in Luther's gospel. But because they used violent methods and didn't respect the God-given vocations of their lords, Luther urged those lords to put the uprising down. When they used even more violent methods than the peasants, Luther was shocked and dismayed.

❸ The marriages of Philip of Hesse.
Philip was one of Luther's most powerful supporters. Philip's wife wouldn't divorce him, and he wanted to make his mistress an honest woman. He decided to commit bigamy to salve his conscience. Luther forgave the bigamy, saying it could be allowed because it put the other woman into a more secure situation. When word got out, it caused a furor.

❹ Indulgences.
The indulgence controversy of 1517 was a pastoral matter for Luther. He believed it offered no true comfort to sinners, so he wrote a set of talking points aimed at promoting a discussion of the situation. We know that document as the Ninety-five Theses, which sparked a theological and political explosion across Europe.

❺ The troubled conscience.
Luther's biggest pastoral dilemma was in dealing with his own troubled conscience. The Roman Catholic Church's theology demanded ever more godly behavior from sinners. Even with his good intentions, Luther knew his own actions could never fulfill God's demands. But Paul's message of justification by faith was a divine word that actually gave Luther what it promised.

HOW TO FOLLOW JESUS AS YOUR PASTORAL MODEL

When looking for a model for pastoral ministry, don't overlook the obvious. Read the Gospels and reflect on principles that were foundational in Jesus' ministry. Consider these:

❶ Take time to pray.
Jesus took time to talk with God to discern God's will for his life and ministry. It's always good to check in with the boss so you know you're on the right track as you do your job. Who knows, God may redirect you from time to time. Read Luke 11:1-13.

Take time occasionally to rest and recuperate from the rigors of pastoral ministry, as Jesus did.

② Don't work 24/7.

Jesus recognized the need for breaks from his ministry among the people. He intentionally made time for rest and sometimes took retreats with his disciples. Read Mark 6:30-32.

③ Don't do it all yourself.

Jesus sent his disciples out to towns and villages to proclaim the coming of God's kingdom and heal the sick. Working as a team was a means and an end, plus they accomplished more than just one person could have done alone. Read Luke 9:1-6 and 10:1-12.

Jesus did unconventional ministry. Consider adding elements of daring to your ministry. While initially scary, coloring outside the lines can be the ticket to activating new ways of thinking that God wants to bless.

❹ Preach relevant sermons.
Jesus used common stories and examples. This gave his preaching relevance for his day. Likewise, use stories that are easy to understand and make sense in your ministry setting.

❺ Face rejection with grace.
When you serve as a leader, some of your ideas will be rejected. You may be tempted to take this personally. Jesus faced much rejection, yet kept his ministry going in spite of it. Jesus knew that leadership often involves rejection and conflict.

❻ Dare to color outside the lines.
Jesus' ministry was cutting-edge. He spoke with the Samaritan woman at the well. He dined with tax collectors. He healed many different people, some on the Sabbath, which angered local religious leaders. He knew that serving God sometimes meant changing old rules. Read John 5:1-17.

❼ Trust God in the face of evil.
Jesus trusted God when he was tempted by Satan. Jesus trusted that God was present and working even during his arrest, trial, and crucifixion. Remember that God is present and working in any and all situations you face too.

HOW AND WHEN TO RESPOND TO A REQUEST FOR PASTORAL CARE

❶ Respond immediately.
Respond immediately to let the person know when you or someone can come. Never answer with a vague "I'll come when I can" or "I'll come sometime."

❷ Respond appropriately.
In cases of critical need, emergency, or death, drop everything and go. You may need to go to the hospital in the wee hours of the morning. Under normal circumstances, let the person know exactly when you will visit.

❸ Consider the location for meeting.
If the person is not in the hospital or in a care facility, consider meeting in your office, in a home, or in a public place. Use common sense and good judgment so the person can feel at ease, but also to safeguard yourself against impropriety.

❹ Know when to refer the person to other authorities.
Don't hesitate to refer to other professionals. In some situations, it is better to use community resources—a member of Alcoholics Anonymous, a social or mental health worker, or a legal person, for example. You are a pastor, not an expert in mental health, legal, or medical issues. Your call is to address issues of faith and faithful living.

⑤ Set good boundaries.

Good pastoral care aims to enable people to stand on their own feet, not become dependent on you. Be sensitive, but set boundaries with people who take unlimited time, often neither wanting nor heeding whatever counsel or advice you might give.

Please Note

- Some of the most important times for pastoral care appear when nobody has requested it. You learn that an individual or a family is in difficulty, and you contact them. Sometimes just being with people will prompt them to go beyond small talk and open up their hearts to you.

- When you become conflicted regarding the best course of action, call a trusted mentor or your bishop for advice, but never divulge what has been told you in confidence.

- Some pastors find a scale system to be valuable. In questionable circumstances ask the person, "On a scale from one to five, how critical is it that I come right away?" Be cautious never to let them hear this as a judgment, but as a valuable tool you use to discern the best way to serve them.

HOW TO MAKE AN EFFECTIVE HOSPITAL VISIT

Hospital visits can deliver enormous encouragement to a parishioner. Consider the following:

❶ Know the general hospital rules.
Be aware of the hospital's visitation hours and special guidelines for visiting intensive-care patients. Stop at the nurses' station before visiting, especially if the parishioner needs to be seen outside of visitation hours.

❷ Make the initial visit.
In most cases, you should keep the initial visit short, obtaining basic information about the patient's condition and saying a prayer for blessing, health, and God's presence. Don't overdo it, especially if the patient is unconscious. More time may be spent with family members as needed for their support.

❸ Plan for any subsequent visits.
Follow-up visits at regular visitation times may be 15 to 30 minutes, depending on the patient's health or rehabilitation schedule. Allow the nature of the situation to determine frequency of visits. When hospital stays are very short, follow-up may be face-to-face or by phone.

❹ If the person is sleeping, err on the side of waking her or him.
When hospitalized, most parishioners want to see their pastor. If you find them sleeping, ask the nurse if it is all right to wake them. If not, leave a card or note and plan to return again soon.

5 Encourage families to talk to the patient (not about and in front of the patient).
Talking to the patient in honest and open ways will help set aside fears. Be mindful as well that seemingly sleeping or unconscious patients often hear and retain conversations.

6 Do whatever possible to give the patient dignity and power.
Lying prone in a hospital bed can be demoralizing and humiliating. Encourage the patient and family members to ask the medical staff as many questions as seem important to them, to insist on comfort and courtesy, and to assert their needs.

7 Offer a closing prayer at the end of every visit.
Before praying, be sure to ask what the patient would like you to pray for. If the patient hasn't already told you all that is on his or her mind, it will come out right here.

Please Note

- Privacy laws limit a hospital's ability to notify a pastor when a parishioner is admitted.

- Use a regular announcement or a note in worship bulletins and newsletters to invite parishioners to contact you or the church office about hospitalizations.

HOW TO MAKE AN EFFECTIVE HOME VISIT

Home visits are important to ministry in many settings. Consider the following:

❶ Call ahead.
Make arrangements for home visits in advance to ensure the times are convenient for parishioners and they will be at home.

❷ Start the visit off on a light note.
Begin home visits by talking about more casual topics before turning to serious business. If a television (or stereo or video game) is on when that time comes, respectfully ask if it might be turned off.

❸ Clarify the reason for your visit.
You may be visiting to get acquainted with a parishioner or family or to talk about membership, a new program, an item of concern to the congregation, or the direction of ministry in your church. If you are there to give pastoral care, allow time for the person or family to talk about the issues. Find out what you or the congregation can do to provide ongoing help or support, if appropriate.

❹ Offer a closing prayer.
At the end of the visit, or if a meal is served, offer a prayer. Before you pray, ask if parishioners have any specific prayer concerns or requests.

Please Note

- In general, limit your visits to an hour or less. If for any reason parishioners aren't feeling well, the visit should be shorter.

- If a parishioner is unable to attend worship with the congregation, consider offering Holy Communion during your visit.

If a television, stereo, or video game is on during a home visit, respectfully ask if it might be turned off.

HOW TO MAKE AN EFFECTIVE SHUT-IN AND CARE FACILITY VISIT

Visits to a parishioner who has difficulty leaving home (who is "shut in") or who lives in a care facility can help keep the person connected to the parish. Consider the following helpful guides.

❶ Consider whether to call ahead.
Making an unannounced visit can give you a clear picture of how a person with mobility limitations is doing in terms of health and living circumstances, but call ahead if he or she has frequent medical appointments. For a care facility visit, avoid coming during the mealtimes.

❷ Arrange to visit shut-ins regularly.
Unfortunately, many people with mobility limitations who live alone or in care facilities do not receive many visitors. Stop by and see them on a regular basis, perhaps for an hour every four to six weeks. Encourage other parishioners to visit as well. Consider a visitation team to supplement your visits.

❸ Bring something tangible to connect the person to your ministry.
Always bring a worship bulletin or newsletter so the person stays connected with parish life. Also offer copies of devotional booklets to encourage daily prayer and reading of Scripture.

4 Talk about the congregation.
Tell the parishioner what is going on in the congregation. Be positive and hopeful. Encourage participation in whatever ways might seem possible. Be sure to request daily prayers for the congregation and its ministry.

5 Ask about the parishioner's family.
Acquaint yourself with their names, locations, and interests and refer to them during future visits. Asking about family members will give you an indication of how much support the person is receiving.

6 Encourage the person to remain as active as possible.
Encourage outings or involvement in activities that are offered in the community or care facility. The more involved people are, the less isolated they will feel, and the better health they will continue to have.

7 Administer the sacrament whenever possible.
Make the Lord's Supper a regular part of every visit, as the parishioner desires and is able. Draw connections with the meal that the whole family of God shares at worship.

8 Closing prayer.
Before praying, be sure to ask what the person would like you to pray for. If the parishioner hasn't already told you what is on his or her mind, it will likely come out right here.

TEN THINGS YOU SHOULD NEVER SAY TO A PARISHIONER

1 "If you're ever looking for some good real estate...."
Some pastors need second jobs. Even so, it's bad form to solicit business while serving as pastor in your congregation.

2 "I don't see your name on any church committees."
This compound guilt-producing statement puts a person on the defensive by assuming far too much.

3 "Thoroughly justified, sanctified, washed clean in the blood of the Lamb."
There's nothing wrong with the ideas, it's just that they are expressed with so much insider jargon that even insiders are likely to get mystified. Communicate to parishioners using immediate and fresh language. Avoid slang.

4 "That was a stupid/dumb/silly thing to say."
Even if you hear someone say something hurtful, this response abuses pastoral authority.

5 "I hate so-and-so."
This contradicts Jesus' command to love our neighbors and will undoubtedly come back to haunt you later.

6 "We have to be strong now." Or, "It was for the best." These hollow responses represent misguided efforts to comfort the bereaved. Such platitudes presume the pastor knows how the griever feels—a faulty assumption.

7 "Just a minute. I need to go talk to someone about something important."
Every person you speak with is made in the image of God. Even a shred of a pastor's focused attention can make a difference, while indifference does silent damage.

Consider carefully whether you want to take
a political stand in your role as clergy.

⑧ "I saw you nod off during my sermon."
First, ask yourself whether your sermon could have been dull. Second, why shame someone who actually chooses to go to church? Be thankful she or he is there—and tell her or him.

⑨ "If you take your faith seriously, you'll vote for...."
U.S. law bans congregations from making political endorsements. Trust that your congregation will vote in a way that honors God.

⑩ "Here's my phone number. I'm free Friday night."
If you are single, use restraint, extreme caution, and care in dating a member of the congregation, lest you become the source of gossip or undue discord. Keep your council president and your bishop apprised of these matters whenever appropriate to safeguard yourself against impropriety.

HOW TO USE THE GRAPEVINE TO SUPPORT YOUR MINISTRY

All congregations conduct some kind of informal grapevine activity. Information passed on the grapevine tends to focus on people, will sometimes be accurate, and will usually have an element of sensation in it. But the grapevine can be a useful tool for ministry if used judiciously.

1 Decide precisely what message you need to get out.
Not all things are worth sending along the vine. Don't overuse it. Important changes, especially those that might garner some opposition, are good candidates.

2 Identify individuals who tend the grapevine.
Some will be have a reputation for knowing what's going on and sharing it. Contact them first. Make them your friends, because you don't want them as enemies.

3 Make sure the word has an element of sensation in it.
The "release" has to focus on people and how it will affect them. It must present something new. For example, "Changing from red carpet to blue in the narthex, as we hope to do, will help calm unruly children before worship."

4 Time the release for greatest possible effect.
It may take a week or so for something to get around the vine, depending on how titillating it is. Allow this time, but not much more. News tends to fade quickly. Take any action associated with your grapevine campaign quickly, before it has a chance to sour.

⑤ Monitor your message's progress by contacting confidantes along the line.

"Did you hear…?" is a good question to use. Listen for distortion or negative spin that might kill the item. Launch a corrective effort immediately, unless you discern an opportunity to use the distortion to your advantage.

Please Note

- Grapevines easily become channels for gossip and can be destructive. Take care not to foster negatives about people or to encourage wagging tongues. Keep the focus positive and the outlook hopeful.

The grapevine can be a useful tool for ministry when used judiciously. But beware its dangers.

HOW TO IDENTIFY A CHURCH ALLIGATOR

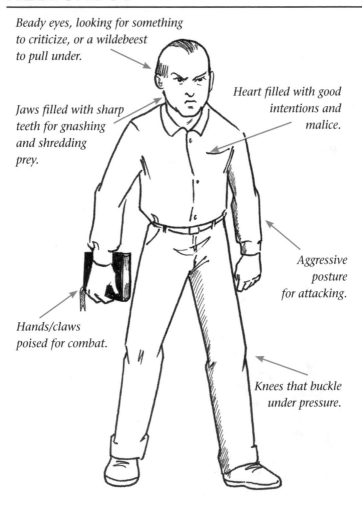

Beady eyes, looking for something to criticize, or a wildebeest to pull under.

Jaws filled with sharp teeth for gnashing and shredding prey.

Heart filled with good intentions and malice.

Aggressive posture for attacking.

Hands/claws poised for combat.

Knees that buckle under pressure.

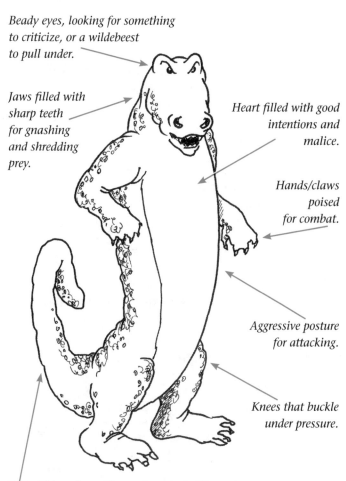

Beady eyes, looking for something to criticize, or a wildebeest to pull under.

Jaws filled with sharp teeth for gnashing and shredding prey.

Heart filled with good intentions and malice.

Hands/claws poised for combat.

Aggressive posture for attacking.

Knees that buckle under pressure.

Tail. (This only applies to the actual alligator.)

HOW TO AVOID GETTING TRIANGULATED

Triangulation occurs when a person is too apprehensive to communicate directly with another person for fear of the reaction. She or he will go to a third party to release this anxiety. This can contribute to the formation of gossip and rumors. Triangulation can also cause conflict to escalate and spin wildly out of control.

❶ Set a good example.
Avoid triangulating others in your congregation or family. If you have a problem with someone, speak directly to that person. Avoid carping and nattering.

Set a good example by training leaders in your congregation to recognize and prevent unhealthy communication.

❷ Remain alert and ask for specifics.
Listen for the words "a lot of people are complaining" or "somebody asked me to speak to you." Follow this up by asking for names. Make it a policy to ignore anonymous complaints.

❸ Find the source and confront. Use love.
If you are given the name of someone who has triangulated you, speak directly with that person. Ask why she or he was afraid to talk to you.

Please Note

- Triangulation in human relationships is common. What matters most is your response.

- The approach your staff and congregation council model sets the tone for how triangulation is viewed in your congregation. Work with leaders to recognize unhealthy communications.

HOW TO MANAGE HABITUAL DROP-IN VISITORS SO YOU CAN GET YOUR WORK DONE

❶ Do Not:
- Run into your office and pretend you are on the phone.
- Exit out a side door as they are walking in the front door.
- Pretend to have a previous appointment.

When habitual visitors drop by the church office, do not run into your office and pretend that you are on the phone.

- Invite them to sit down with a bowl of candy and encourage them to finish it.
- Ignore them.
- Throw yourself on the ground in a mock temper tantrum.
- Drop everything to converse with them.

❷ Do:
- Politely greet habitual drop-in visitors and check how they are doing, even if it is a brief conversation. A very brief conversation.
- Acknowledge other commitments on your schedule and indicate the amount of time you might have for a visit (allowing the person to get to the point of the visit).
- Maintain healthy boundaries at all times.
- If habitual visits become irksome, probe for possible underlying reasons behind them: loneliness, crisis, pending decisions, curiosity.
- Consider finding a task for them to perform and involve them in positive activities around the church.
- Give thanks that the church is considered a safe place to linger.

HOW TO REMAIN CALM IN A CRISIS SITUATION

A leader is often defined by the way he or she behaves in times of crisis. Clear, deliberate thinking and decisive action can prevent further damage or distress and return a sense of order. Here are some tips to remain calm in a crisis situation.

1 Pray.
Whenever circumstances permit, gather all concerned into a circle of prayer. Anchor your petitions with words like "patience," "providence," "calm."

2 Breathe deeply.
Deliberately force yourself to take at least three deep breaths in a row. Don't allow your body's adrenal reaction to dominate you.

3 Clarify. What is the crisis?
Ask questions and wait for complete answers. Avoid acting on inaccurate or incomplete information.

4 Assess whether any persons are in danger. If so, respond quickly.
Utilize any appropriate emergency resources at your disposal.

5 Trust in God's guidance to lead you through the crisis.
This can provide the greatest sense of calm within your person that gets communicated through your actions.

Please Note

- It may be helpful to make a list of potential "first responders" (parishioners who are medical professionals and those trained in CPR and first aid) in case of a medical crisis at a congregational gathering.

- In the event of a disaster situation in or near your community, a pastor can play a key role in identifying needs, recruiting volunteers for relief work, or comforting people in temporary shelters.

HOW TO PREPARE MENTALLY FOR A FUNERAL

Funerals can be the hardest part of parish ministry. Generally, the longer a pastor serves a parish, the more difficult some funerals can be because of the pastor's close ties with the people.

❶ Spend as much time as is appropriate with the family. Tell stories.
You may be with the family in their home or in the hospital soon after the death. Help them talk about the deceased person, any of his or her congregational activities, and any favorite hymns, Bible passages, or stories of faith. Tell stories and encourage the family to share memories, too. Pray.

❷ Gather your resources prior to the funeral.
Gather the family around the coffin for a prayer and further sharing of memories. This again will be hard, with tears often flowing freely (the family's and maybe yours), but it will prepare the family and you for the visitors, phone calls, and condolences that will be coming in the next hours.

❸ Remain focused and professional during the service, but allow yourself to reveal real emotion.
The concentration of leading the service may carry you through without breaking down. If you are concerned about this, have an assistant standing by to perform parts of the liturgy for you. Keep a handkerchief or tissues and a glass of water handy.

Please Note

- If the deceased is a member of your own family, take your place with the grieving family. Do not attempt to preside. In such cases, it is appropriate for you to speak on behalf of the family, but allow a colleague to officiate at the service.

SEVEN PREACHERS IN THE BIBLE AND WHAT MADE THEM GREAT

❶ Paul.

Paul was the greatest preacher to the Gentiles. He saw everything and spoke every word in light of the cross. He said to the Philippians: "I regard everything as loss because of the surpassing value of knowing Christ Jesus my Lord. For his sake I have suffered the loss of all things, and I regard them as rubbish, in order that I may gain Christ" (Philippians 3:8).

❷ Moses.

Moses was not an eloquent speaker, but his brother Aaron spoke on his behalf. Moses is remembered as the law-giver, because God gave the law through him. But for Moses, it was crucial to speak the truth no matter what the cost. Moses had to speak the truth to Pharaoh (Exodus 5). Moses had to speak the truth to the Israelites (Exodus 17). Moses even had to risk all and argue with God! (See Exodus 32.)

❸ Joshua.

When Joshua was called to replace Moses as Israel's leader (Joshua 1), God told him to be "strong and courageous" (Joshua 1:6). Joshua was, and he understood the paradox of the faith: that we are unable to be faithful to God even as God is always faithful to us. Joshua called the people to follow God and at the same time warned them that they were not capable of following God: "You cannot serve the LORD, for he is a holy God" (Joshua 24:19).

4 Mary Magdalene.

Mary Magdalene, the "apostle to the apostles," was the first to whom Jesus appeared after his resurrection (John 20). She did not recognize him at first, but when he called her by name, she knew him. Jesus gave her the message that she was to bring to the disciples, perhaps the very first sermon. She went to the disciples and announced, "I have seen the Lord" (John 20:18).

5 Hosea.

Hosea lived the message. God told him to marry a woman who would be unfaithful to him and have children with her. Hosea obeyed to live out the message that Israel was like Hosea's wife, unfaithful to God. Hosea gave his children symbolic names, including, "Not Shown Mercy" and "Not My People." Like other prophets, Hosea did not receive a warm reception from the people, but he lived the message nonetheless.

6 Isaiah of the Exile.

The anonymous prophet who spoke the messages found in Isaiah 40 to 55 often is called "Isaiah of the Exile" or "Second Isaiah." This prophet's task was to preach hope to a people who had given up hope. Isaiah was a virtuoso and his instrument was the Hebrew language. His poetry is among the most beautiful in the Bible. His words created faith where only despair had existed.

7 John.

The evangelist who wrote The Gospel of John is referred to by that name, even though this may not be factual. John was a master of symbolism. When he retold stories about Jesus, he reclothed the simple stories in elegant symbolism.

Please Note

- All of the preachers in the Bible were great only because God made them great. As Paul wrote of his own ministry, "I planted, Apollos watered, but God gave the growth" (1 Corinthians 3:6).

HOW TO PREACH A PROPHETIC WORD WITHOUT GETTING FIRED

According to Jesus, the reward of a prophet was to be hated, excluded, insulted, and rejected (Luke 6:22–23). And indeed, that is how most Old Testament prophets were treated. But if keeping a job is still important to you, here are some guidelines about how to preach a prophetic word.

❶ Make a searching and fearless inventory of your character.
In the words of Jesus, you are a scribe trained for the kingdom, called to bring out of the biblical treasure what

The authority for preaching comes from the Word, not from you. Hide behind the Bible.

is old and what is new (Matthew 13:52). Remember: In the Bible, the self-appointed prophets were always the false prophets.

❷ Hold the Bible out in front of yourself, not vice versa.
The authority for preaching comes from the Word, not from you. Tell people, "I don't like what this says any more than you do (even though you actually might), but this is what it says, and I am called to preach what the Bible says and not what I like. If you don't like it, take it up with the Lord."

❸ Avoid preaching your own politics.
Whatever you do, do not confuse preaching a prophetic word with blasting the congregation with your political views. A wise teacher once said, "If you like the prophets, then you don't understand them." Likewise, if you like everything you are preaching, then you are not really preaching a prophetic word.

❹ Seek a masterful grasp of law and gospel.
Martin Luther said the sign of a "true theologian" is one who can rightly distinguish law and gospel. A prophetic word will most likely function as law in both the first use (ordering creation) and the second use (driving people to Christ for mercy).

THREE JOKES FOR USE WITH CHURCH CROWDS

1 A couple had been debating buying a new vehicle for weeks. She wanted a fast little sports car to zip through traffic around town. He was looking at beat-up old trucks. Everything she liked was way out of the price range. "Look," she said, "I want something that goes from 0 to 100 in just a few seconds. Nothing else will do. Christmas is coming, so surprise me." For Christmas he bought her a brand new bathroom scale. Nobody has seen or heard from him since.

2 Signs, Signs, Signs

- on a septic-tank truck: "Yesterday's Meals on Wheels"
- on a plumber's truck: "Don't sleep with a drip. Call your plumber."
- on a plastic surgeon's office door: "Hello. Can we pick your nose?"
- on an electrician's truck: "Let us remove your shorts."
- In a nonsmoking area: "If we see smoke, we will assume you are on fire and will take appropriate action."
- on a fence: "Solicitors welcome! Dog food is expensive!"
- in a veterinarian's waiting room: "Be back in 5 minutes. Sit! Stay!"

❸ Did you hear about the little child who came home and said her Sunday school teacher, Mrs. Jones, had "no morals"? The alarmed parent called the pastor to come over. The child repeated the charge.

"Why do you say Mrs. Jones has no morals?" the pastor asked.

The child answered, "Because our last teacher always ended the Bible lesson by saying, 'The moral of the story is...,' and Mrs. Jones doesn't."

HOW TO PREACH A STEWARDSHIP SERMON WITHOUT SOUNDING LIKE YOU ARE BEGGING FOR A RAISE

The route to a faithful stewardship sermon is the same as the route to any faithful sermon—be biblical. Many pastors rank stewardship at the bottom of their list of favorite sermon topics because preaching on money too often feels like saying, "The church needs your money so I can get my annual raise." Help is on the way. Stewardship can move up on your list when the focus is on God's Word.

1 **Focus on the need of the giver to give, not the need of the church to receive.**
The Bible seldom mentions the need of the temple or the church to receive. Rather, the focus stays on the giver's need to give. Giving is an act of worship that acknowledges our dependence upon God. Generous giving is an act of discipleship.

2 **Focus on money's inherent threat.**
The Bible recognizes that money has the potential to be a huge roadblock in one's relationship with Jesus, who says, "You cannot serve God and wealth" (Matthew 6:24; Luke 16:13). In a land of so much affluence, preachers and their listeners need to take this seriously.

3 **Focus on money's inherent opportunity.**
Jesus provides us with an incredible promise when he says, "For where your treasure is, there your heart will be also" (Matthew 6:21; Luke 12:34). Money has the ability

to lead the heart. When we give generously to Christ's mission, we embrace Jesus' promise that our hearts will be led to him as well.

Please Note

- When a stewardship sermon is grounded in God's Word, it will encourage growth in relationship with Jesus and will not be a pitch for a raise.

When a stewardship sermon is grounded in God's Word, it will encourage growth in relationship with Jesus. It will not sound like a pitch for a raise.

HOW TO CREATE A CLIMATE OF CARE, LOVE, AND OPENNESS IN YOUR CONGREGATION

God calls, gathers, and sustains people to be the body of Christ, inspired and ignited by God's own Spirit, so that the climate in a congregation reflects God's tremendous and expansive love. Unfortunately, a congregation can grow inward, becoming ensnarled with inner conflict or stagnated by apathy. How can a congregation instead nurture a climate of care, love, and openness?

❶ Creating a climate of care.
Encourage and equip members of the congregation genuinely to care for one another. That means:

- Taking time to get acquainted with one another.
- Listening to one another's stories, including sharing pictures of key people in one another's lives (such as children, grandchildren, and great-grandchildren).
- Taking great interest in the children and youth of the congregation and following their sports, concerts, and activities.
- Sending notes and cards to one another (especially at key times in life).
- Visiting one another in the hospital or in times of need.
- Thanking one another for the ways each offers gifts and talents to the building up of the body of Christ.
- Laughing with one another.

❷ Creating a climate of love.

To develop a climate of love, point to God's love made known in Christ. God first loved us, so we respond with lives of love. Allow God's love to come through the congregation as the congregation becomes an instrument of love. Help everyone in the congregation to learn to love God, others, and themselves. That means:

- Being still, prayerfully pondering God's love for you and the congregation and ways to share God's love with others.

- Praying for a loving heart.

- Praying for those with whom you have difficulties (as well as for your enemies).

- Praying for people as they come into worship or as they take communion.

Study all of the congregation's publications.
Would visitors feel welcome to participate?

- Praying for people who are sick, shut-in, or otherwise in need.

- Praying for the leaders of your congregation, including the staff.

- Praying a blessing for each person you meet.

- Watching how God uses you and the congregation to create a contagious climate of love wherever you go.

❸ Creating a climate of openness.
To develop a climate of openness, invite several non-members to come to your congregation on a variety of Sundays. Ask them to share their observations with you. Use this information tenderly as you seek ways to guide your congregation to become more open. That means:

- Praying, privately and publicly, for God's Spirit to open your hearts.

- Opening your routines and inviting neighbors to come and worship.

- Opening your eyes to exclusivity (in-house language) in your church bulletin, newsletter, and Web site. Do your publications invite visitors to participate?

- Opening your ears to new hymns. Select music to attract a variety of ages.

- Opening your minds as you listen to others. Find a way to agree to disagree, yet remain connected as the body of Christ.

- Opening your hands and seeking ways to serve, breaking down barriers of poverty, prejudice, and injustice as you reach out in the name of Christ.

HOW TO CONDUCT YOURSELF AT AN ECUMENICAL WORSHIP SERVICE

While ecumenical worship presents a wonderful opportunity to glimpse faith in action beyond the walls of your church and denomination, it also presents special challenges for decorum.

❶ Refrain from judging the customs and rituals of other faith traditions.
Scripture reminds us, "Do not judge, so that you may not be judged" (Matthew 7:1). Moreover, it is impossible to achieve the right frame of heart and mind while maintaining a critical stance. Avoid gasping at foreign practices, especially when your microphone is turned on.

❷ Follow Christ's example of servant leadership.
The Son of God was not beyond washing his disciples' feet, which were almost certainly repugnant in the extreme. In similar fashion, seek opportunities to serve an ecumenical gathering with a glad heart and with humility. Any use of hand sanitizer should be done in private.

❸ Search for and celebrate common ground.
The ideal ecumenical service allows diverse people to unite in a larger community. The best way to facilitate this—especially in a sermon—is not to wrestle over differences, but to find points of belief all can embrace. Try not to draw attention to an ecumenical colleague's "funny

hat" or "maniacal hand-raising," for example, in cases where these are present.

Please Note

- Don't just mind how you act, but how you react! If anyone at the service seeks confrontation or causes friction, take the high road with humility. A show of grace under pressure is priceless testimony.

HOW TO DEAL WITH DISGRUNTLED TRANSFERS FROM OTHER CHURCHES

❶ Plan ahead.
Anticipate the reality that such disgruntlement will occur. Work with other clergy in your area to decide how you'll handle these situations.

❷ Keep the Eighth Commandment.
Speak positively of the former congregation and its pastor, for Jesus is also present where two or three or three hundred are gathered in his name.

❸ Notify disgruntled transfers that the grass is brown over here too.
Your congregation is filled with sinners just like the last place. If they think they're about to enter a place without brokenness or hypocrisy, they just haven't gotten into the thick of things yet.

❹ Consider asking questions that focus on Christ's benefits for sinners.
- "How do you think life among this gathering of sinners will be different from the place you're leaving?"
- "What does it mean to you to be a part of Christ's body?"
- "What did you experience in your old congregation that told you of God's mercy for a sinner like you?"

5 Send them home with an assignment.
Indicate to them they must seek a transfer from the pastor of the congregation they're leaving. Give that pastor the opportunity to provide pastoral care to these sheep.

6 If the transfer papers come, meet again and talk about involvement in the congregation.
Infer the mutual burden of establishing trust. You have responsibility for the wider health of the congregation. Be aware that past disgruntlement is a good predictor of future dissatisfaction, but be clear also that fresh starts can mean new life.

7 Pray openly with the transfers to bless and christen the new beginning.
Name these sinners before God and ask your Lord to make you into a faithful preacher for their sake.

HOW TO DRINK COFFEE

❶ Understand the implicit goal involved.
The purpose of drinking coffee is not to drink coffee but rather to visit with a parishioner. If you like good coffee or need the caffeine, consider patronizing a place that specializes in coffee. If you don't like coffee, you can still accept an invitation to share a cup of coffee with a parishioner, because the goal is the relationship.

❷ Attend to your posture carefully.
There are two basic postures: standing and sitting. (In either case, there is something for your whole body to do.)

To assume the sitting posture for drinking coffee, roll your shoulders, slide your bottom forward, and stick out your legs. In other words, forget all rules of good posture and try to slump.

Sitting: Despite what your mother told you, try to slump. Roll your shoulders, slide your bottom forward, and stick out your legs. Place a paper napkin in your lap. In one hand, hold the cup. (Paper, foam, plastic, and porcelain are all acceptable cup varieties.) In your other hand, hold a "goodie." (Doughnut holes, bars, cookies, and cake are all examples of acceptable goodies.) Make eye contact. Also, it is acceptable to talk with your mouth full. Disregard the crumbs. Messiness will endear you to your audience.

Standing: This usually occurs in a church narthex or fellowship hall. Notice how many people you are visiting with and form a loose circle. Allow a comfortable distance

Drinking coffee and eating goodies while standing is a formidable challenge. To survive this situation, remember that the goal is to visit with parishioners. The coffee cup and goodies are simply means to this end.

between speakers (never less than a foot [30 cm], rarely more than three feet [90 cm]). Adjust the circle as people come and go. Hold your coffee in one hand and a goodie in your other hand.

❸ Measure your intake. Consider rationing.
Church coffee is generally weak, so you can drink it all day and still remain calm. A "cup" is generally three-quarters full. A "half cup" generally is one-third full.

❹ Obey the time-tested rules of etiquette.
In the case of a home visit that involves coffee, it is customary for hosts to apologize for what they are serving you. They might say, "Sorry that I don't have very much to offer" or "Sorry that these cookies didn't turn out just right." This is not a sign the fare is of poor quality— rather, it's an invitation for you to compliment the host.

HOW TO ACCEPT COOKIES AND OTHER GOODIES GRACIOUSLY WITHOUT GAINING WEIGHT

Parishioners love to grace their pastors with leftovers following potlucks and cookie fellowships. These tend not to be carrots and peas, but foods with the highest calories and fat content. Consider these ideas for accepting leftovers graciously without expanding your waistline.

1 Use good political sense.
If you value your call and peace within your congregation, remember that it is not wise to refuse leftovers from a parishioner. Such refusals will always be perceived as rude and insulting to one's cooking.

2 Accept all offers of free food.
Smile when asked if you would like leftovers. Then as inconspicuously as possible, retrieve the empty containers that you have prepared in faith for this moment. Accepting it does not mean you must consume it.

3 Use moderation.
Don't be greedy and choose your own leftovers and their portions, lest you be perceived as a boor. Instead, allow the parishioner to guide you. Take some, refuse others, as befits the model of moderation in everything. This will help your reputation as a pastor as well as your waistline.

④ Attempt to mitigate any false perceptions on the part of the cook/server.

If you truly have a dietary restriction on a particular food item, be honest about saying so. Most parishioners will know this already, since you are part of a church family

> *Don't attempt to eat all the leftovers given to you by parishioners just because the food is there. Eat in moderation and freeze the rest for future eating (in moderation).*

that cares about your health and other good gossip. Accept a substitute that is not restricted. When receiving something you detest, refer back to principle 2.

⑤ Share your booty with others. Avoid foisting bad food on family.

Hoarding your leftovers is a sure way to gain weight. Therefore, share your treasure with other members of your family. If this isn't possible, share with your friends and those who come to your door for help. Reserve the parts you like best for yourself. Give the food you detest to your dog. If you don't have a dog, give it to the neighbor's dog.

Please Note

•   When all the above fail and your waistline increases anyway, take the last resort: diet and exercise.

HOW TO LISTEN TO THE SAME STORY FOR THE 100TH TIME AND FEIGN INTEREST

❶ If you are hearing the same joke for the 100th time, but from a new person

Many people think that pastors like Bible jokes and don't realize that you have heard them all before. (For example: "Where is baseball mentioned in the Bible?") Here are two strategies:

a. *Laugh.* Fake a laugh and say, "No matter how many times I hear that joke, it is always good."

b. *Add to it.* Chuckle mildly and say, "If you like that one, you should also know that baseball is mentioned in Genesis 2: Eve stole first, Adam stole second, and later they were both thrown out."

❷ If the same person is telling you a personal story for the 100th time

Many people tell the same one or two stories at every Bible study, coffee hour, and committee meeting. Here are two strategies:

a. *Play bingo.* Make a bet with a friend about which story the person will tell first. If you win, shout, "Bingo!"

b. *Ignore it.* Let the person finish and then continue on with the meeting as if she or he hadn't said anything.

HOW TO RESPOND WHEN YOU FORGET A PARISHIONER'S NAME

It happens to every pastor and terrifies every pastor—forgetting a parishioner's name. There are some things you can do to minimize the horror.

❶ Conjure up a nickname.
Say, "Good morning, chief," for example. This works best if you regularly use nicknames for people. Other options: governor, boss, friend, and *compadre*.

Consider carrying a small supply of name tags and a marker with you at all times. When you forget a parishioner's name you might suggest they put one on "for the sake of visitors."

❷ Haul out a biblical name.

Example: "You know, you always remind me of Barnabas, because you are so encouraging." Then call the person Barnabas for the rest of the day. Other options: Martha (hard worker), Jonathan (good friend), and so on.

❸ Get them to share their name through subversive means.

Example: "Say, I want to call you about something later, can you write your name and phone number on this piece of paper so that I don't have to look it up?" Be sure to call them about something later.

❹ Deliberately use the wrong name but deny it.

Example: "Good morning, Chris." When they correct you say, "What did I call you? I was just thinking about Chris and I must have misspoken."

❺ Be direct and honest.

Example: "I can't remember your name, can you remind me, please?" There is something to be said for being honest and not playing any games.

FOUR WAYS TO HANDLE THE TACKY GIFTS THAT PARISHIONERS GIVE YOU

All pastors feel for you in this situation. We are all in this together.

❶ Designate a special area of your desk for tacky gifts.
When a tacky gift donor is coming over, quickly display the appropriate gift in this prominent spot.

Downside: You may forget to switch, you may receive a surprise visit, and you may confuse who gave you what.

❷ Designate an entire room for tacky gifts.
When you receive a visit from a donor, spend time with the person in this room.

Downside: You may not have the luxury of an extra room that can be set aside for this use.

❸ Designate a specific wall for tacky gifts that hang.
This is similar to the room strategy, except it uses a wall.

Downside: Many gifts you will receive such as "praying hands" and other statues and figurines cannot hang on a wall.

4 **Relinquish your entire office for the display of tacky gifts.**

Keep all of your gifts in your office at church. If you are married, your spouse may favor this solution.

Downside: The number of tacky gifts in your possession could multiply. Your parishioners may see your display of gifts and assume that your taste matches the gifts.

The Spot for tacky art.

Tacky art to hang on The Spot when the giver visits.

WORSHIP STUFF

TEN THINGS YOU SHOULD NEVER SAY DURING WORSHIP

❶ Say nothing your grandmother wouldn't want to hear.
One day you'll stub your toe or drop the bread while your microphone is switched on. Prepare for those times by never using vulgarities—even in private.

❷ "If you're visiting, please stand and introduce yourself."
The surest way to repel newcomers is to embarrass them. There are better ways to welcome visitors.

❸ "I hope you don't (cough-cough) catch my cold."
If you're sick, don't cough into the microphone, and keep your mitts off the Communion bread. Better yet, stay home and get well.

❹ Never call the printed Order of Service a "program."
Concerts and ballgames use "programs." Call it a "worship folder" or a "bulletin."

❺ "Let's give the (choir, Sunday school teachers, or kitchen workers) a round of applause."
Say instead, "Let's thank God for them." Then everyone can applaud God. Worship, after all, is praising God. Plus, saying, "Thank God for you," is more meaningful to a volunteer than "good job."

6 **When preaching, never tell a story about yourself unless it's intended to illustrate sin.**
Being the hero or martyr in your own story just doesn't work. Your congregation knows you too well in all likelihood for you to pull it off, anyway.

7 **"Personally, I'm voting for..." or, "As a Christian, you should vote for..."**
The worship service should focus on what God has done and is doing, not on your political positions.

8 **When leading prayers, don't say, "I just really want to praise you, Lord."**
You're praying on behalf of the community, so it's appropriate to say "we" not "I." Further, "just really want to" sounds canned.

9 **When leading praise-style worship, don't say, "The next song we'd like to do is...."**
You'll sound like a nightclub singer. The noun *song* comes with a useful verb: "We'll *sing* our next song."

10 **"Happy birthday!"**
Personal stuff makes insiders feel fuzzy, but it also creates outsiders. Worship isn't "family" time; it's public time. Save birthday wishes for the fellowship hour.

Please Note

- Announcement time is the riskiest occasion for saying something you wish you hadn't. "Off-the-cuff" quickly turns into "foot-in-mouth." The cure is simple: write your announcements and greetings, and stick to the script. Keep it short. Less is more.

HOW TO WELCOME VISITORS

1 Do not:
- Ignore them. Visitors aren't toothaches. When you ignore them they DO go away.
- Ask them to sit in the front row of the sanctuary. Allow them the option of anonymity for a comfortable interval.
- Make them feel guilty if they do not join the congregation.
- Place them on committees as a way for them to grow in Christ.

2 Do:
- Receive them with open arms and encourage members of the congregation to do the same.
- Pray for them throughout the week.
- Introduce them to others in the congregation who might share similarities.
- Invite them to other activities at the church.
- Smile when you see them and welcome them.
- Offer to assist them in any way.
- Visit them in their homes to become better acquainted.
- Celebrate the habits being formed as they return again and again.
- Expect and monitor their growth and activity as disciples of Jesus Christ.

HOW TO USE YOUR FAMILY MEMBERS AS SERMON ILLUSTRATIONS WITHOUT ALIENATING THEM OR BORING THE CONGREGATION

A pastor in a congregational setting may preach more than 50 sermons a year. Finding illustrations for this many sermons may be difficult. Using family members as sermon illustrations is tempting, but must be done with care.

❶ Avoid embarrassing stories.

Don't use an illustration that makes fun of a family member. That's asking for trouble. Consider each person's personality characteristics. Remember that telling even positive stories may embarrass family members if they are shy.

❷ Avoid inappropriate topics.

Some subjects are inappropriate for sermon illustrations. Avoid details about your spouse's or family members' personal and intimate health issues.

❸ Ask permission before involving a family member in your public work.

When in doubt, ask your family member if you can use a story. Explain the connection between the story and the text. If he or she does not understand the relationship, the story may have been a bad illustration from the start.

④ Focus on the Scripture passage you're preaching.
A gospel message based on the text for the week is the main thing you want to communicate in a sermon. The illustration should promote and further explain the gospel message. If the illustration overpowers the gospel message, don't use it.

⑤ Consider fictionalizing the story.
Change the names in the story. Change some of the other details. Present it as a fictionalized illustration. This will protect your family from possible embarrassment and still permit you to draw on your life experiences in a creative way.

Avoid embarrassing your family members before the congregation with personal stories that may offend them. Repairing a relationship damaged in this way may prove difficult.

⑥ Get feedback on your sermons from family members.
Ask for feedback on your sermons from people you trust.
Ask what they like and what you might do better. This
could be risky. You could also learn a lot about how
others perceive your preaching style.

Please Note

• Supply pastors may feel more secure using family illustrations because the family member retains anonymity.
  Proceed with caution anyway.

HOW TO PREACH WITHOUT NOTES

Preaching without notes requires a different mental process than manuscript preaching, but it can be learned in steps. Many pastors who thought it impossible are now doing it regularly.

❶ Shift from a manuscript to a brief outline.
Write your manuscript as you normally would, then identify the "blocks" or "moves" in it. Leave the opening and closing paragraphs so you know how to begin and end, but condense the remainder down to one word for each block.

Preach without notes to avoid the perils of the manuscript shuffle.

② Move from a brief outline to a list of words.
When you become accustomed to an outline, condense the opening and closing down to one word each. Now you're preaching from a list of approximately 20 words. Write that list on a small piece of paper.

③ Dispense with the written list; commit it to memory.
When you're able to keep the list of key words in your head as you preach, you're ready to preach without notes.

Please Note

- Don't fret if you forget parts of your sermon when you preach without notes. Think back to your key words and keep going. Note: A short list is easier to remember.

- The ability to preach without notes gives you the option to deliver your sermon outside the pulpit if you wish. Start outside the pulpit by carrying a list of key words with your Bible, then move to no notes.

- As with all preaching styles, the key to preaching without notes (and preaching outside the pulpit) is "practice, practice, practice." Go over the sermon out loud until you are confident you know it. Practice in front of a mirror or on tape to evaluate your delivery and fine-tune your style.

HOW TO WING A SERMON WHEN YOU FORGET YOUR NOTES AT HOME

Just because you misplace your notes doesn't mean you've misplaced your knowledge of outstanding sermon architecture.

❶ If there's time during the opening portion of worship, draw up a rough outline on an index card centering on a theme.
Many thematic touchstones have timeless power to touch worshipers: forgiveness, perseverance, possibility, hope, community, or courage in trials.

❷ Study the Scripture lessons and urge the congregation to place themselves in the story.
With the story of Mary and Martha, for example, ask rhetorical questions that force listeners to consider who they identify with—the "doer" or the "dreamer." Or, if recalling Christ's Last Supper, ask which apostle they could see themselves as and why.

❸ Try recalling your sermon highlights and see what might fit into your winged version.
It's likely you'll remember certain passages from your text precisely because they were worth remembering. Search for the emotional emphasis and reclaim the passion from the missing script.

❹ Consider venturing into the experiential.
You don't need your notes to paint a picture with words—engage the congregation in the sights, sounds,

smells, and textures of the Bible, or your subject matter, to the point where they can feel themselves placed into the scene.

⑤ Pray, pray, pray.
This is not about you. You are spreading good news that has been around 2,000 years. Trust that God, who led the Israelites out of captivity and raised Jesus from the dead, will bring you through this minor ordeal.

⑥ When all else fails, employ the "Moses rule."
Moses was not known for his silver tongue, but spoke powerfully before Pharaoh on behalf of his people. He trusted that when he opened his mouth, God would give him the right words at the right time.

Please Note

- No one has ever complained that a sermon was too short.
- Consider using a winged sermon as an opportunity to work on your use of the dramatic pause.
- Focusing on a single theme or Scripture verse can yield great fruits in an extemporaneous atmosphere.

EIGHT COMMON HAND GESTURES USED IN PREACHING

1. The wagging finger indicates scolding on the part of the preacher. It's better to let the law show sinners their true state than for the preacher to use this gesture.

2. The pounding fist is generally used as a last resort to shake up unrepentant sinners who have inoculated themselves against the law.

3. The precise okay says, "I am now making a very particular and nuanced point that I worked hard to come up with in my sermon preparations."

4. The pulpit grip demonstrates a lack of confidence and comfort in the word being preached or in the relationship with the hearers. (The parallel for non-pulpit preachers is wandering aimlessly from place to place in the chancel while preaching.)

5. The hoisted text says, "God said it. I believe it. That does it." This gesture reveals a reluctance to trust the preached word over against the written word. It's better to preach law and gospel in a way that shows their power and truth to actually make new people out of sinners.

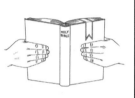

6. The hand of blessing, when used properly, conveys the power of God's blessing much like a superhero shooting a beam of light from his palms. It bestows Christ's benefits "for you."

7. The heartfelt tap indicates a tender moment or the authenticity of the gospel for sinners.

8. The sweeping hand represents either our common sinfulness or the fact that Christ's mercy is "for you."

Please Note

- Body language involves more than your hands. Pay attention to your stance, posture, and movement during the sermon.

- The size of your gestures should be balanced to the size of the room, the size of the preacher, and the importance of the point being made.

- Be careful about accessorizing beyond wearing a stole. You don't want to inhibit the movement of your hands or take the focus away from the divine word being preached.

- Profane hand gestures are never appropriate in worship.

NINE USES FOR OLD SERMON MANUSCRIPTS

❶ Reusing.
You can reuse old sermon manuscripts (hereafter, OSMSS) when you give devotions at the nursing home.

❷ Recycling.
Use the back side of your OSMSS for confirmation lessons and committee minutes. Keep a recycling basket under your desk.

❸ Packing.
Save OSMSS to use as packing material when you leave your current call.

❹ Giving.
If a parishioner compliments you on a sermon, present that OSMS to him or her as a Christmas gift, suitable for framing.

❺ Leveling.
Many parsonages are old and lack level floors. You can fold up OSMSS and place them under the corners of shelves, tables, and desks to reduce instability.

❻ Helping.
When confirmation students hand in sermon notes that indicate a certain degree of inaccuracy, give them the appropriate OSMSS and suggest they take another try at it.

❼ Lining.
OSMSS work well as drawer liners. Place them facedown to avoid soiling a manuscript you might use later. Other OSMSS can be used to line bird cages and cat boxes.

❽ Protecting.
OSMSS can serve as splat mats for art projects during vacation Bible school and finger painting bibs for young children.

❾ Preserving.
If you or your spouse enjoy scrapbooking, use decorative scissors on the edges of OSMSS. This will preserve them for your golden years. You will be shocked that you ever preached such heresy.

Please Note

- To reduce the volume of OSMSS, use a smaller font, smaller margins, smaller spacing, and fewer words.

Old sermon manuscripts make excellent packing material when you leave your current call.

HOW TO RECOVER WHEN YOU LOSE YOUR PLACE OR FORGET DURING A PUBLIC PRESENTATION

You're reading, preaching, or presiding when all of a sudden you lose your place. Or the worship service is moving along and you realize you skipped a portion of the liturgy. What can you do?

1 Be prepared.

Good preparation reduces the chances of losing your place or skipping part of the worship service. Stash extra copies of the bulletin everywhere you expect to be during the service. Place a bulletin in your hymnal too. Then walk through the service in advance so you and others know exactly what you're doing.

2 Keep calm. Don't let on you're lost. Maintain a sense of intentionality.

This projects an air of confidence and control. When something like this happens, don't panic. You may feel embarrassed, but parishioners will take it in stride.

3 Take a prayerful moment to reorient yourself.

Calmly get your bearings. This is usually sufficient for finding your place again in a reading, sermon, or liturgy. If a portion of the service was skipped, evaluate the missing part. If it is absolutely necessary, insert it as soon as possible. If it is not absolutely necessary, leave it out.

❹ Move on.
Every pastor has been in this situation. Don't dwell on it, and the congregation won't give it a second thought either.

Please Note

- If you lose your place often due to insufficient preparation, the congregation will conclude that you don't take worship seriously enough or that you're entering your dotage.

- The decision whether to insert a portion of the service that was skipped should be based on liturgical and theological importance (if there is confession of sins, there should be absolution, for example), along with a sense of church relations (don't leave out an announcement from the council president, a solo, or a choir anthem).

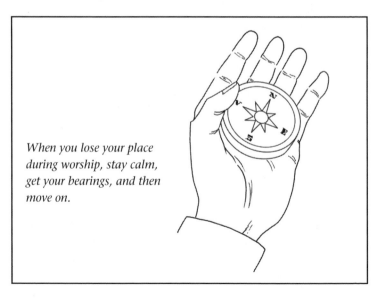

When you lose your place during worship, stay calm, get your bearings, and then move on.

HOW TO RECRUIT WORSHIP ASSISTANTS DISCREETLY WHEN SOMEONE DOESN'T SHOW UP

Involving lay people in worship develops leaders and enhances attendance figures. But sometimes worship assistants fail to show, and you need a quick recruit. The best method depends on the role that needs to be filled.

❶ For help distributing bread or wine:
- During the opening hymn, when everyone is standing, sidle over to a proven congregational leader and ask for help.
- Whisper. Everyone likes being whispered to by the pastor.

❷ For help collecting empty communion cups:
- Simply make eye contact with a fifth- or sixth-grader and beckon. They'll come up eagerly.
- Reward them by whispering a compliment or something funny.

❸ For help reading the Scripture lessons:
Unless you can quickly identify and recruit a go-getter lector you know won't mind, fill in and do this yourself. Most people prefer to practice.

❹ Don't worry about ushers.
Ushers never miss. Directing traffic, passing the plate, scanning the crowd from the back—it's the coolest job. In the unlikely event that an usher doesn't show up, consider calling the missing person's name forlornly from the chancel with your brow furrowed—while peering toward

the rear of the sanctuary—until a substitute volunteers out of sheer pity.

Please Note

- Thank your "pinch hitters." Catch them after church or drop them a note: "I knew I could count on you." Consider sending them a gift certificate to their favorite fast-food restaurant.

- Check on the one who did not show up. No scolding, only concern.

Recruiting someone to collect empty communion cups takes very little effort. Simply make eye contact with a fifth- or sixth-grader and beckon. This method generally produces the desired result.

HOW TO HANDLE A RINGING CELL PHONE DURING WORSHIP

Modern-day technology requires new vigilance on the part of worship leaders. Posting signs at the entrance to your worship space, noting the prohibition against cell phones and pagers in your bulletin or projected on your worship screen, and making verbal announcements as worship begins can all help ward off embarrassing incidents. But occasional cell phones get through.

❶ Equip ushers with squirt guns.
Many older gentlemen appreciate a John Wayne-style gun belt to accompany their six-shooter. Younger ushers prefer Super-Soakers.® Keep towels handy to dry the offender off and avoid hard feelings.

❷ Sing along with the ring tone.
Consider asking the organist to play along, then extemporize a hymn or praise song that utilizes the tune.

❸ Stop suddenly in mid-sentence and give the offender the most withering look you can summon.
The longer you hold the stare, the more uncomfortable everyone will become.

❹ If all else fails, simply allow the moment to pass without pause and assume that the person is fallible, is heartily sorry, and will try not to let it happen again. This approach is preferred by worship leaders and pastors who want to remain employed.

If a cell phone rings during worship, consider singing along with the ring tone. Be prepared. Program your own cell phone to play "A Mighty Fortress Is Our God."

HOW TO HANDLE LOUDSPEAKER FEEDBACK

The most important thing about loudspeaker feedback can be summed up in this age-old proverb: "An ounce of prevention is worth a pound of cure."

❶ Stand behind the "speaker line."

Keeping your microphone behind loudspeakers will eliminate a primary source of feedback.

Loudspeaker feedback during worship is disruptive. Take all preventative measures to avoid it.

❷ Make sure speakers are not pointing directly toward your microphones.
Moreover, never point microphones toward any speaker.

❸ Purchase an equalizer for your sound system.
Perform a sound check prior to a service. Turn the volume up and listen for where feedback begins. "Wooo" feedback is a bass frequency, while a "screech" is in the treble end. Use the equalizer to turn down the offending frequency.

❹ Employ a person trained with sound troubleshooting during the worship service.
Having someone else do this is much easier than trying to do it yourself.

If you've done all this and feedback happens anyway:

❺ Do not cup your hands around the microphone capsule.
This only promotes more feedback.

❻ Turn off your microphone at once and reposition it in a safe location.
In the event this fails, consider using your own voice as a substitute. Project your voice with pressure from your diaphragm.

❼ Turn down the volume on the sound system.
This will stop most feedback. Gradually raise volume to a level below the point where feedback started.

HOW TO RECOVER FROM AN OPEN-MIKE GAFFE

A microphone can save your vocal chords and help people hear you better. While overcoming self-consciousness about wearing a mike is a worthy goal, don't forget about your mike altogether. It could be on at a time when you would rather not have anyone hear you. If such a gaffe occurs, follow these steps:

❶ Avoid apologizing repeatedly for technical malfunctions.
If it's outside your control, don't apologize. This includes shorted lead cords, malfunctioning mikes, planes flying overhead, passing locomotives, and the like. Rather, keep going with even more energy. The congregation will see— and appreciate—what a trooper you are.

❷ Make light of noticeable errors.
Allow minor slips to pass, but you may want to acknowledge the larger boo-boos with a funny story or self-effacing joke afterward. This will show the congregation how warm and funny you are.

❸ Apologize for any major blunders.
Words picked up by an open mike can't be taken back. If the words are offensive, rude, or disparaging, an apology will be in order. The congregation will see how human and imperfect you are, in case they needed a reminder.

Please Note

- Always remove or switch off portable microphones when you visit the restroom.

- Many lavaliere-type microphones have miniscule on-off-mute switches that tend to hide in the folds of an alb or underneath a suit jacket. Take the time to position these so you can reach the switch easily, even if it means an obtrusive battery pack.

- For extreme misstatements that are job-threatening, consider claiming cell phone or CB radio interference. Divert attention away from yourself.

HOW TO RESPOND TO A SHRIEKING CHILD INCIDENT

A wailing child will distract you from leading the liturgy, praying, or delivering your sermon. An outburst may cause others to squirm, disrupting the entire worship experience.

1 If this is the first time the child has disrupted worship, choose one of these options:

- Ignore the interruption, carrying on as if you didn't hear.

- Respond to the interruption by signaling an usher to invite the parent and child to the nursery, or slowly move toward the child yourself, giving the child attention and

When a shrieking child interrupts worship, signal an usher to invite the parent and child to the nursery. Never, under any circumstances, signal surrender.

showing concern for the parent. Quietly suggest that the child needs some personal care right now.

- Defuse the tension with humorous words or sermon illustrations. The child may calm down when everyone else relaxes. If not, the parent and child can slip out of the sanctuary during the laughter.

❷ If this is an ongoing problem, suggest alternatives with the parent or guardian.
- Use the church nursery during the quiet parts of the service. Allow the child to worship with the congregation through the active times.

- Recruit another adult or teenager to help with the child.

- Invite the parents to sit toward the front. Sometimes being closer to "the action" helps children become more engaged.

- Provide a "worship bag," a cloth bag for each child, filled with small quiet toys, a child's Bible picture book, crayons and paper, and nutritious snacks.

Please Note
- Train your ushers to respond to these incidents as quickly and quietly as possible, whenever they can.

FIVE COMMON WEDDING FAUX PAS AND HOW TO AVOID THEM

Weddings generate happiness, joy, and awe as two people stand together in God's presence. Still, weddings also generate pressure and stress. Pastors can deflate matrimonial jitters by properly handling these five potential pitfalls.

❶ Insensitive sermon icebreakers.
Let the best man and maid of honor dish dirt during reception toasts. Avoid untoward joking about in-laws, how the bride and groom met (especially if it involves illicit or embarrassing behavior), premarital counseling conflicts, or starting a family.

❷ An obnoxious videographer.
A frantic or obtrusive videographer can make a wedding seem more like a crime story on the evening news. Frenetic rushing robs the ceremony of its sanctity. Issue clear instructions to the video crew—both at the rehearsal and before the ceremony—to remain out of the way and move through the sanctuary in measured paces.

❸ Inaudible, rushed, or botched Scripture readings.
Coach readers to maintain a constant distance of three inches (7.5 cm) behind the microphone, taking care not to turn their heads or crane their necks down suddenly, which cause sound dropouts. Have them read from double-spaced, typed text instead of a small-print Bible. Urge readers to practice until they have memorized most of the passage.

❹ Cheesy, obscene, or otherwise inappropriate music.
Many couples choose to honor friends by asking them to play or sing at their ceremonies—not realizing that often, these people may lack experience in a live setting. As early as possible in preparations, make sure musicians familiarize themselves with the selections they'll perform. A good general rule is: Don't save the music until the last week! Make sure backing tapes, if used, are properly cued and that the sound system is in working order.

❺ General awkward moments.
The average cost of a wedding in the United States in 2005 was almost $26,400, according to CNN. For many couples, that's a sizeable investment into making sure the details of the day go just right. You can do your part during the ceremony in any number of areas—from subtle coaching of bridal party members to having a hankie handy in case the bride or groom gets weepy (or worse, succumbs to a very runny nose).

HOW TO SURVIVE AN ANXIOUS BRIDAL PARTY

❶ Know your role.
The pastor is not a hired wedding coordinator but a public proclaimer of God's Word called to a particular congregation. You have the job of making sure even a wedding service is done in a way that those present hear law and gospel in their truth and purity.

❷ Work with your congregation's leaders in advance.
Have your congregation council, music staff, and wedding coordinator develop clear guidelines for couples to use in planning their wedding.

❸ Define the wedding service clearly.
- Christian congregations want to take every possible opportunity to give Christ's benefits to sinners, including those who want to be married.

- A wedding, just like Sunday morning worship or a funeral service, is a place for the congregation to make sure God's Word is brought to bear on sinners' lives.

- Thus, a wedding worship service is provided by the congregation to couples being married. It's not something couples pay for.

❹ Expose couples and their families to a new vocabulary.
In working with a couple before the wedding, give them language that will define their lives together differently than this month's issue of a bridal magazine. That may mean speaking about the difference between a wedding

and a marriage, how sin reveals itself in relationships, and how Christ uses spouses to pass his undying mercy to each of them.

⑤ Be willing to run interference.
Sometimes circumstances arise in which neither the bride nor the groom can control the situation. You may be called on to be the voice of the law by delivering a clear "no drinking or inappropriate behavior" speech at the rehearsal, not letting a controlling parent wrest the focus from God's blessings in the service, or making sure members of the bridal party pay proper respect to the church building itself.

⑥ Preach toward the marriage rather than the wedding.
Betrothed persons may have utter confidence in their own ability to create lives for themselves. Thus, whatever else is said, you will need to focus on a future time when the gift of family will become a burden and when Christ's forgiveness will be the element that makes the present day's promises take effect.

PERSONAL STUFF

HOW TO RECOVER FROM CHRISTMAS AND EASTER OVERLOAD

Responsibilities for parish pastors increase prior to Christmas and Easter. There are usually additional worship services and social and family functions that demand your time and energy. Recognize that you need time for rest and renewal.

❶ **"Layer" your activities during crunch times.**
When a visit with a parishioner and, say, your exercise schedule conflict, consider inviting the person to accompany you on your run or trip to the gym.

❷ **Schedule activities that recharge you.**
Consider your personality. Are you energized by being with people? If so, spend time with family and friends. Do you need time alone? If so, seek solitude. Spend time on hobbies. Build this need into your weekly schedule and adhere to it.

❸ **Avoid neglecting your vacation time. Consider scheduling time off immediately prior to or after Christmas and Easter. Relocate geographically.**
Recovery involves removing your daily mind-set from work and into a completely different set of concerns. Replace the stress-inducers of daily ministry with simple problems, such as which roller coaster to ride or which fishing rod to use.

4 Plan for your time off at the same time and in the same fashion as you do major holidays, to give them equal status in your mind and on your calendar.

5 Count your blessings.
Many pastors are so focused on the details of worship preparation they can't hear the gospel message for their own lives. Take time to consider the blessings in your life. This may include skipping worship while on vacation.

Recovery from Christmas and Easter overload is aided by diversions into hobbies and such.

Please Note

- Planning ahead to lighten your other responsibilities during busy times speeds recovery.

- If you decide to take a week off following Christmas or Easter, seek pastoral and supply preaching coverage several months in advance. This will ease your stress level immediately prior.

HOW TO STAY FIT

Long hours, late-night emergencies, traveling (especially if you have a specialized ministry or are on synod or church-wide staff), and high job stress can take their toll on your health. You need to take a holistic approach to your health and attend to all your needs—physical, emotional, social, vocational, intellectual, and spiritual. If one area is out of balance, it affects the others. Good stewardship requires attention to maintaining a balanced life.

❶ Care for your body. Make this a regular priority.
Pay attention to your optimum weight and body mass. Watch your diet and eat more vegetables and fruits.

Even the most effective ministry can benefit by the pastor staying physically fit and emotionally sound.

Exercise on a regular basis. Get regular physical checkups. Monitor your stress levels.

❷ Attend to your emotional well being.
Pay attention to changes in your emotional and mental health. If friends or family comment that they see negative changes, listen to them. Seek medical attention to rule out an illness that could affect your emotional well-being. Seek a counselor or therapist if stress levels get too high.

❸ Schedule time for friends and family. Allow this time to push aside work-related duties occasionally.
Do not omit the social aspect of your life. Whether single or married, develop a network of friends with whom you can relax and be yourself. Get together on a regular basis.

❹ Live life with purpose.
Develop a mission statement for your life, then follow it. Recognize and acknowledge your unique spiritual gifts. Use them in all aspects of your living.

❺ Practice lifelong learning.
Education is a lifelong process. There is always something new to learn. Develop your strengths and attend to your weaknesses. Read books and view movies that interest you, not necessarily all related to theology.

❻ Develop spiritual practices.
Pastors who conduct worship services may have difficulty finding spiritual renewal and refreshment themselves. Take time to meditate and pray. Seek new spiritual practices that feed you.

Please Note

- You are a human being and therefore are susceptible to colds and acute illnesses. Your genetic makeup also plays a part in your physical and emotional health.

- An occasional indulgence in things that are bad for you, such as a forbidden meal, can make staying on a diet long-term more productive. Do not allow the rigors of staying fit to overcome you.

- Fitness is a work of the law by which you are not saved.

HOW TO ESTABLISH AND MAINTAIN THE DISCIPLINE OF DAILY DEVOTIONS

One of the most effective ways to establish and maintain a discipline of any kind is to make it part of a daily routine. The same is true of the discipline of daily devotions.

1 Read the Scripture. Consider reading schedules that move you through the Bible in a year's time.
Allow for your own personal encounter with God's written Word. Mornings, when you first awake or first arrive at your office, are often good times for devotions.

2 Reflect on the Word as it pertains to your life, personally.
Consider how the metaphors, insights, judgments, and mercies in the words you read impact your own soul and psyche. This will become the fertilizer for future sermons and pastoral acts.

3 Pray.
Take time to communicate with God through prayer, naming those who are dear to you, those who are in need, and those who suffer; lifting up your own needs before God; and giving thanks for blessings of all kinds. Consider keeping a written or typed list that you update daily or weekly.

❹ Repeat the process daily.
Read, reflect, and pray each day, until you can't leave home in the morning or turn off the last light at night until you've taken time for daily devotions.

Please Note

- A variety of materials and methods can enrich your daily devotions. Explore various devotional resources from a variety of writers, write your own devotions, reflect on the poetry of hymns, or sing your prayers. Reflect and pray on themes you find in newspapers, movies, books, music, and other art forms.

- The first days of establishing a routine are the hardest. Hang in there!

- If you realize one day that your routine has fallen apart, don't give up. Read, reflect, and pray that day, and the next, and the next.

- It's easier to maintain a routine if you are accountable to someone else. If you are married, consider sharing daily devotions with your spouse. If you are single, you might seek out a prayer partner or spiritual director.

HOW TO KEEP UP ON CURRENT TRENDS IN THEOLOGY, EVEN WHEN YOU'RE BUSY

What fitness enthusiast, amateur athlete, or hobbyist would take up a hobby or sport but never practice? If you're really dedicated to something, you'll find ways to "stay in the game"—even when you're busy. The same can be said of those dedicated to the practice of theology. Here are some ideas that may help you.

❶ Seek the partnership of stimulating thinkers, including nontheologians.
Doing theology is communal work. Find partners with whom you can do theology. Consider other clergy. Don't overlook ecumenical partners and the countless lay theologians—members of your own congregation—you rub elbows with.

❷ Subscribe to a trade journal or two.
It's hard to follow every development in theology. The articles and book reviews in theological journals are great overviews and they'll point you to further resources for deeper exploration.

❸ Reading is work too. Count it as work hours.
Make a habit of assigning regular reading times to yourself. Don't wait for someone else to give you permission.

④ Pay attention to what your parishioners are watching and reading.

Your parishioners depend on you to help distinguish between the wheat and the chaff. Be their resident theologian.

⑤ Draw up a three-year plan for continuing education that strikes a balance.

Get to know folks at the lifelong learning centers, seminaries, and colleges. Work with them to plan regular surveys of the theological landscape. Keep your involvement broad, too, by pursuing nontheological courses and self-education.

⑥ Get out of town.

A theological education event, movie, and dinner at your favorite ethnic restaurant may be just the adventure you're looking for. If you're married, don't forget to invite your spouse occasionally.

HOW TO MAINTAIN A SOCIAL LIFE AS A SINGLE PASTOR

Members of your congregation may respond with frantic matchmaking efforts on one hand, or the assumption that you are available to the congregation at all hours on the other hand. These suggestions can help you maintain a healthy, sane, and fulfilled life as a single pastor. Balance is the key.

1 Find out where your social peers spend time. Don't ask your parishioners for that information.

2 Accept invitations to occasional meals and celebrations at parishioners' homes.

3 Visit coffee shops, bookstores, or parks where you can meet people who aren't members of the congregation. Avoid lurking or the appearance of lurking. Don't write

When you meet people outside your congregation, don't try to break the ice with a quick confession of sins and absolution.

off parishioners as potential friends, but remain hyper-vigilant regarding appropriate boundaries.

④ Engage in hobbies that bring you into contact with adults not associated with your congregation.

⑤ Consciously open yourself to meeting new people, either on your own or through others.
Introverts especially should make an intentional effort in this area. Don't go on every date proposed by every well-intentioned matriarch of your church. Beware of the political minefields involved.

⑥ Set clear boundaries for hours you are available, both in and out the office.
Don't allow others to assume that no spouse or children means that you don't need personal time.

⑦ Frankly inform people you meet outside of church about your vocational path.
Responses will vary, but disingenuousness is always the wrong approach. Don't try to break the ice with a quick confession of sins and absolution.

⑧ Avoid flaunting in front of married people the personal flexibility that a single life allows you.

Please Note
- Remember that only you can perform effective self-care. If you need greater private time or thrive on social inter-action, set those standards for yourself.

HOW TO KEEP BOTH YOUR JOB AND YOUR FAMILY

It is possible to set and maintain healthy boundaries between work and family so that one does not adversely affect the other. Boundaries are the key.

❶ Leave work problems at the office.
Avoid complaining or talking in great detail about work at home. Complaints may cause your family to become angry with the people who upset you. This is not healthy for anyone.

❷ Leave your family problems at home.
Avoid sharing family problems with coworkers or congregation members. They may find this annoying. Share only enough to let colleagues and staff know what's going on.

❸ Encourage the congregation to have realistic expectations of your family.
Remind the congregation that when you were called as pastor, your family was not "hired" to fill empty leadership positions. Your family members may participate in the activities they choose.

❹ Honor your Sabbath.
Don't skip days off or vacations. Publish your day off in your congregational newsletter so members of your congregation will know when not to bother you for non-emergencies.

⑤ Make family life a priority.

Spend the majority of your time off with your family. Eat meals together. Laugh and play together. If you have children, spend time with them. Avoid sowing the seeds of future regrets.

⑥ Maintain a social life outside of the congregation.

Make sure that your idea of a family dinner out is not the monthly potluck dinner at church. Do things together that do not involve members of your congregation.

Please Note

- Some specialized ministries demand lots of travel and time away. It will take more effort on your part to stay connected with your family. Use e-mail and instant messaging to keep in touch.

- You set the boundaries and tone of the relationship between your family life and your work. If you do not honor your family, your work won't either.

> *Making family life a priority sets good boundaries and a good example for your parishioners. Defend your family time with vigor.*

FIVE WAYS TO HELP YOUR MARRIAGE THRIVE DESPITE THE DEMANDS OF THE JOB

Helping a marriage thrive while meeting the many demands of pastoral ministry is a challenge. Here are some ways to do this if you are a married pastor.

❶ Schedule devotional time with your spouse.
Each day, read and discuss Scripture and pray together. Schedule this time in advance, and make it a part of your daily routine. Purchase a devotional book for couples, decide to read a particular book of the Bible by chapter, and so on. Hold each other accountable to taking time to do this every day. Lift each other up in prayer during your devotions and at other times during the day.

❷ Date your spouse.
Schedule time to enjoy fun activities or special places as a couple. Plan a surprise afternoon, evening, or weekend away with your spouse. If it helps, establish a weekly "date night" and keep it religiously.

❸ Take time off with your spouse whenever possible.
Shared relaxation is critical to an enduring marriage. Spend quality time together renewing and recharging. Rearrange your schedule so your down time overlaps.

❹ Collaborate to set boundaries.
Decide together on boundaries between your work and your time together as a couple. During mealtimes, you might have an answering machine pick up non-

emergency calls. Limit the number of evenings you will be at church each week. Identify which types of marriage responsibilities "trump" church responsibilities. Determine how much "church talk" you will allow during the time you spend together.

⑤ Take "time-outs" when needed.
Agree that you or your spouse can call for an immediate time-out if schedules or the demands of the job get out of control. If a time-out is called, discuss what's happening and how you will respond together. Speak the truth in love. Set expectations for change, and respectfully hold each other accountable to them.

Learn from the sports world. Call for a "time-out" with your spouse when the demands of the job get out of control. Discuss what's happening and how the two of you will adjust the game plan.

HOW TO AVOID ANSWERING PERSONAL QUESTIONS

As a pastor, you will know some of the most intimate details of people's lives. You will hear about their struggles, pains, and joys, and they may want to reciprocate. This is not appropriate. It blurs the boundaries between the roles of pastor and people, and places an unfair burden of confidence on them. Here are some ways you can create appropriate boundaries:

1 Avoid depending on your congregation to meet your emotional needs.
Find friends and colleagues you can confide in instead. When your stress levels exceed the normal range, seek counseling.

2 Avoid spending all your time at the church.
If you practice your own Sabbath time, the congregation will realize that the church is not your whole life. This will encourage respect of your personal life and your time.

3 Acknowledge their concern.
Some people may ask you inappropriate questions because they genuinely care about you. Don't get angry with them for that.

4 Change the subject.

5 Set clear boundaries.
If someone persists in asking personal questions, tell him or her that you feel uncomfortable responding.

Please Note

- Clear boundaries do not mean you must never empathize out of your own experiences with people who might benefit. This should, however, be kept within the context of pastoral care.

HOW TO GET OUT OF A TRAFFIC TICKET

1 Plan ahead.

Most police officers are deferential toward clergy. If you can't always wear your clerical collar when driving, wear it for your driver's license picture. Consider handing the officer your business card with your license. Be advised that the latter tactic may be perceived as fishing for

Plan ahead. Always wear your clerical collar when driving.

leniency and cause the reverse effect. Clerical collars are proven to be more effective.

❷ **Behave in a dignified manner or a manner befitting common preconceptions about clergy.**
Over-apologize. Compliment the patrol officer on his or her sharp nylon shirt and shiny badge. If you've popped out your clerical tab while driving, pop it back in quickly. If you're chewing gum, spit it out. Pitch your voice low. Address the officer as "my child."

❸ **Be patient.**
Don't rush to assume the worst before you hear it. Let the officer speak before you do. Furrow your brow in concentration as you listen.

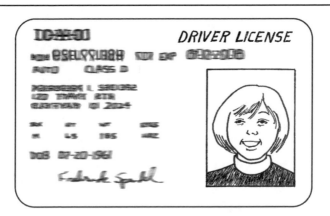

If you can't always wear a clerical collar while driving, wear one for your driver's license photo. Please note: Have a backup plan in place. Thou shalt not depend solely on a driver's license mug shot to get you off the hook.

❹ Confess your wrongdoing openly and honestly.
When you are told that you've been clocked at such-and-such miles (or kilometers) per hour over the speed limit, admit your guilt as sincerely as possible.

❺ Show sincere contrition.
Honesty is more effective with penitence. Admit that you were wrong and also promise reform—at least for this trip.

Please Note

- Some officers think it their duty to punish clergy. If one of these is at your car window, pray fervently.

THE PROS AND CONS OF WEARING A CLERGY SHIRT

Cons:

❶ You run the risk of looking officious.

Others may think you're all about the power and authority of your calling. Certain persons will believe this regardless of the truth.

❷ They're designed to be uncomfortable, compared with your other shirts.

Some manufacturers use cotton in their pastoral garb products, which won't wick away perspiration in a non-air-conditioned sanctuary on a Sunday morning in July. Many use polyester, which wicks away moisture but over-insulates, so you sweat more to begin with.

Pros:

❶ You can easily disguise your utter lack of style.

Not having to coordinate colors and patterns prevents you from offending others' fashion sensitivities.

❷ You can often gain access to otherwise off-limits locations to bring God's promises to sinners.

The collar (sometimes in combination with a clergy identification card from the synod office) can allow you to make a pastoral visit to a prison or hospital when a T-shirt wouldn't.

❸ You are marked as one leashed to God's Word.

The clergy shirt tells everyone (including you) that you occupy the office of pastor. You don't speak your own opinion, but do so on God's behalf. Avoid pontificating.

Please Note

The service of ordination says a Lutheran wearing a clergy shirt is responsible for the following:

- Preaching and teaching in accordance with the Scriptures, the church's creeds, and the Lutheran Confessions.
- Studying God's Word and using the means of grace.
- Praying for your people and nourishing them with God's Word and the sacraments.
- Providing an example for your people in your upright life and faithful service.

*The clergy shirt tells everyone (including yourself)
that you occupy the office of pastor.*